James A. Whitney

Shobab

A Tale of Bethesda

James A. Whitney

Shobab
A Tale of Bethesda

ISBN/EAN: 9783337120016

Printed in Europe, USA, Canada, Australia, Japan

Cover: Foto ©ninafisch / pixelio.de

More available books at **www.hansebooks.com**

SHOBAB:

A Tale of Bethesda.

A POEM.

BY

JAMES A. WHITNEY, LL.D.

NEW YORK:
N. TIBBALS & SON,
124 NASSAU STREET.
1884.

TO THE MEMORY OF MY FATHER,

AMAZIAH WHITNEY,

WHO DIED THIRTY YEARS AGO.

A MAN OF KINDLY HEART AND GENTLE WAYS,

WHO, FROM YOUTH TO AGE,

FEARED GOD AND KEPT HIS COMMANDMENTS.

THIS VOLUME

IS REVERENTLY INSCRIBED.

SHOBAB:

A TALE OF BETHESDA.

I, Shobab, son of Shimei who wed

The day the tidings unto Hebron came,

That in the mouths of the high caves of Seir

The Hebrews laid dry fagots, and with fire

Slaughtered the mountain robber in his den—

Tell this my tale, now that the years remote

Seem near again, as seems the desert path

Kenned from the height that marks the journey's
    end

Through sunset's level light.

That winsome day
Joy ran in rivulets within each heart,
As wine flowed from the beakers to the lips
Of all the village; while triumphant notes
Swept from the harp's strained strings. The war-
　　horse loosed
Sprang with proud curvet in the pasture field,
Hearing the distant cymbals' lordly clang
And challenge of the shawm on free winds blown.
That day was peace. The ox freed from the yoke
In comfort all unwonted chewed the cud.
White patient flocks along the wayside grazed
The bitter herbs, contented; and the dove
Beneath the eaves cooed loving notes and low.
Upon the springing wheat the sunshine lay
And o'er it swept the shadows of the clouds.
The grass gave forth the murmur of the bee,
From winding brooks came rustle of the reeds,
And from beneath the reeds the monotone
Of rippling waters. And anon, the shout

Came ringing far, of those rejoicing loud
That from Seir's caverns nevermore should reach
The ruffian hordes to spoil the quiet land.
And with it mingled on the breezy air
The rhythm of the songs that graced the feast,
Of this the marriage afternoon, when all
Was joyousness of triumph, and of love.

The sun sank from the zenith and its ray
Was followed by the dusk on gliding wings.
The soft night followed dusk with gentle feet
As maidens chase the brown moths mid the ferns.
Upon her head the stars came forth and shone;
The cool breeze from the mountains swept her hair,
For this the gray clouds seemed; and every breath,
As from her lips, made murmuring soft and low.
Yet on and on the cymbal and the lute
And voices shrill and sweet together swam,
Now high, now low. And everywhere the mead
Poured slow and luscious; and the sparkling juice

Of Hebron's trodden grapes made glad the hour;
Until the coming of the morning star
Beheld all slumber-vanquished; all save where
A slender ray shone on the glistening cup
Where the glad bridegroom pledged the smiling bride
In one last draught ere tender sleep should come.

Late the next morning to their tasks afield
Went laborer and master; for the joy
Was gone its way, and life began again
Its old accustomed course. The day and night
Came, blessing, each in turn. And seasons bore
Each in its turn the burden of its time.

So triple threefold months went calmly by:
And joy unto that dwelling came again.
Not clamorous as before but all subdued
To soft low spoken words and tenderness;
When to my lips they pressed the honey-comb

And on them, drop by drop, laid spicéd wine,
Hushing my cry with gently jangled songs
Breathed pleasant, low, and sweet.

          This have I told
As long thereafter it was told to me,
For I knew not the passing of the years,
Until it happened that the women cried,
And all the children silent gazed in awe
The while, swart armed, the toilers from the field
Bore to our door a Roman soldier, dead;
A sickle's jagged thrust across his neck
And his bright cuirass dabbled with his blood.
Then hue and cry there was that quick my sire
Should die the death. But Roman vengeance knew
No slaking of its thirst; for he was gone
Unto the farthest nations of the east
And never more Judean hill or vale
Or wife or child beheld. My mother told
Me how the hireling cursed him. Him, who sprang

From out the branch of Jesse.   Him whose sires
Had seen the glory of the Lord anear.
The Roman smote him.   Him, a Hebrew, born
Heir to the glory of this ancient land,
Son of its kings who ruled o'er all its plains
Ere yet the distant marshes spawned the crew
Whose sons on Judah laid their heavy yoke.

On, through succeeding years that drowsy crept;
With sorrow dull'd, and with dull'd labor cold,
We two, alone, a humble shealing held,
The mother and the child.   The reapers knew
Our loneliness and woe and careful laid,
As if unheeding, little gavels down
That we might find them as we gleaned the field.
And here and there when olive branches gave
Their last yield to the press, was fruitage still
A willing guerdon to our anxious quest.
And so we dwelt, the mother and the child,
Seeing the springtide and the harvest come

To Hebron's fertile fields and go away
And come again. And I grew on, apace,
Dreaming and wondering of the weary world.

He who hath seen the cedars on the hills
May call them to his eye when they are gone.
Though of the meads that charmed him, nevermore,
Of slender grass-blades kens he any one,
So much alike were they and small to see.
Thus, seven things, to me, of all those days
Are clear as sight of cedars 'gainst the sky,
Though all the rest be faded.

                                      I recall
That by the wayside once a woman laid
A brown hand on my head, for she was swart
As the ripe olive's husk—a little child
Clung to her garments, and with curious eyes
Looked up into my face—to me she spake:
Oh, child, but thou art fair to look upon,

And innocent thine eyes, and soft thy voice;
Therefore, I would the marvels that I work
May bless thee in the passing of thy days,
That whom I love may blessèd be through thee.
Take then these seeds. Aye, in mine own far land
The stately symmetry of Theban palms
Have I beheld, when peace and rest were mine.
And may they spring from out these kernels dark
To wave o'er thee in peace ere yet ye die;
So plant them when thy sorrow comes to thee,
For they bear charm of many a prayer deep breathed,
In olden rites the living Lord hath blest.
And water them as to thy burning heart
Ye would the coolness of great calm should come.
The three brown seeds I clasped and she was gone.

Once, in the dark, my mother crooned a song,
And slowly on her knee, the while she sang
She rocked me to and fro. Oh, Father, hear
Thy loved ones of the earth and take them home,

That they no more may know the Winter's cold
Or weariness of Summer's wanton heat,
The toiling of the Springtime, or the wrath
Of sullen Autumn's storms; or any more
The touch of fear on night and morn and noon.
There they may rest, and there, perchance, may sleep
Withouten dream or any thought of toil,
Of sorrow, or of pain. 'Twas then I asked:
Where is this home?

                      And low she answered me.
These bodies that we have are but the bud
That holds the odor of the fruiting flower,
And when it dies the perfume vanishes
But does not die, but lives within the air.
Our spirits pass into a world beyond
Those distant hills, yea, far beyond the sky,
And there they shall have rest forevermore;
The peacefulness of all the flowers that lie

In Summer in the meadows; all the joy
The bees in Springtime know amid the trees.
And it shall be forever—for the just,
The merciful and pure shall enter in;
And we shall rest. Yea, we shall rest, she said.

The while she spake, the crescent moon came forth,
Casting faint shadows on the stubble ground,
And shining on her face. Then was she still,
Saying no more, though waiting patiently,
I listened for her words till wonder grew
And fear came on me at the peacefulness
That spread upon her forehead. Long I watched
Until afield the reapers came again
In the glad morning sun. And she was dead.
With scanty rites they laid her in the ground
And heaped the earth above her, by the road
The camel drivers traverse, leaving me,
Unnoting that I lingered. Then I thought
Of the dark woman's words; and of the seeds

Laid one upon the mold and pressed it deep
With weak, tired fingers, weeping all the while
That she was gone from me. Three times I brought
From the cool spring and three times watered it.
So, ere my task was done, the twilight came
And night wherein I slept and half forgot,
Then woke to weep again.

                Then mourning days
And sad months measured their slow length along
With gradual lessening of the grief they bore.
Each day brought less of sorrow, for it dies
Of its own languishing. And memory knows
Surcease in labor, and in weariness,
Till like an evanescent shadow seems
The presence of our woe. So thro' slow lapse
Came calmness and content, and I was fain—
After forgetful years had come to me—
To sing among the reapers: for I learned

With them to wield the sickle with a hand
Grown deft and strong.

      Yet solitude to me
Threw glamour o'er my heart. I sought the vales
By rugged paths that led to meadows bright
With flowery garniture and slender grass
That gave its dusty blossoms to the air
Ere tiny seeds were ripe. There came to me
Each song the wild bird whistles in the dusk,
Or carols at the dawn. I sought the glades
Where feeble conies bide among the rocks.
I marked the lichens on the boulder stones
Rear little purple cups, and wondered oft
Why sought they not the richer mold below.
I loved the color of the wayside blooms
Softened by evening's gray and tender light,
And fragrant in the early falling dew.

The torrents change their courses in the glens
 And firm rocks deeper groove beneath the storms,

The tow'ring tree grows hoary with the years
And time unmakes the contour of the fields.
But ever breezes blow as in the time
When all the earth was young; and fares the same
Each little wild flower by the wayside grown.
So, when on heart and brain are furrows found,
Long wrought by tempests that are stilled and gone,
Waft memories cool and fragrant as the touch
Of zephyrs born of sunset, and the scent
From springing trefoil in the herbage brown.

So I recall from sunset haze remote,
From scenes of summer blossoms, and the stress
Of gently blowing winds on herb and tree,
A little maiden's face; a child she was
Of soft unconscious grace and tender ways.
Yea, younger than myself, and innocence
Shone in her eyes and her fair forehead crowned.
And all things pure and stainless seemed to me
To be her kindred in the earth and air.

I met her in the fields. We chased the bees,
White-faced and droning, from the thistle tops.
And wove, of golden daisies, slender chains
Wherewith to coil her shoulders. Flame-winged moths
And dotted butterflies to deck her hair
We caught with nimble fingers and fleet steps.
And hand in hand we heard the mavis sing
His welcome to the night, when shadows deep
Of hasting daylight wasted into dark.

From this, our earliest greeting, came the course
Of many eves succeeding. And the tale
For each was like the other. In the fields
The springing blade changed into slender spire;
And swaying spire grew stately in the breeze
With golden stem and gently nodding head.
And from the springtide to the harvest time,
Each twilight like the other in the joy
Of love unsullied and of innocence.

The love of youth is gentle, and its touch
Is like to that which once the prophet's staff
Gave to the brackish springs of Jericho,
Beside whose brink no tender herbage grew,
Or palm bore fruitage, or fair wild bird sang.
Till suddenly, beneath a holy hand,
The bitter waters changed, and clear and sweet
Flowed o'er the barren sands till they were clad
With waving growth of green, wherein the buds
Drooped lowly and unkenned; wherein the blooms
Sprang bright and glorious from the hidden buds;
Wherein the slender shafts of tufted trees
Rose skyward from the flowers; and grateful shade
Was where the aridness of dearth had been.
So in my heart grew gentleness and trust
And fervor for well doing all my days.
Until it seemed, could I but see the ark
Within our Lord's great temple, and behold
The seven stems that waxen candles bear,
That they may light the altar, I would hail

For her and me a life new born and fair,
To reach out through the years in peacefulness.
So when the harvest ended; now, I said,
I will go thither to Jerusalem,
Shall see its marvels and return to thee,
To tell them all unbidden.

                              So I went
And all the wonders saw. But they are hid
Behind the memories of nearer years.
All, saving this, a narrow pool that lay
Beneath high dusky arches where the shade
Was cool while yet the lurid sun was high.
A pool around whose edges threads of green
Lay tangled in loose skeins of slimy drift;
Above whose lazy ripples spiders swung
Aloft on tiny ropes of gossamer
That shone and vanished and then shone again.
While on the sullen waters pillars threw
Broad bars of shadow. Quick my questioning

Was answered by a beggar at its edge.
Why comest thou, the hale, the young, the strong,
And in mid afternoon. The stricken comes
At early daybreak when an angel stirs
To sudden frenzy all the waters calm.
And he who touches first the fleeting foam
Is healed of all his trouble. Go thy way,
This place is not for thee.

                        Chilled as with fear
I quick departed. But my fancy drew
Within my brain the picture of a form
Benign of countenance, and stately clad
In stainless linen that unto his feet
Swept down in folds majestic, while his hand
A sceptre held wherewith to move the pool
To merciful unrest when earliest ray
Of morning sunlight glinted on its breast.
This day-dream dreamed I on my homeward way,
For now three days were vanished and my heart

Said haste to Hebron, for she waits thee there
With welcome on her face. The sunshine fell
And faded in the gloaming, and the moon
The transient twilight followed with no break
Or interlude of dark. In silver light
Was silence as of sadness everywhere.

Twixt midnight and the dawn, upon my couch,
I sought for sleep in vain. For sorrow seemed
To lie upon the air, a hazy woe
That had no object yet was ever near.
When weary I arose, I, unsurprised,
In groups saw all the neighbors speaking low
Among themselves, as if in wrath and fear.

And when I asked, they answered, knows't thou not
The widow's daughter, yea, the little maid
That met thee in the fields, is slain and all
Her blood is mingled with the ashen earth.
A Roman charioteer drove idly by

And seeing her sweet beauty, called to her;
Whereat she fled. Then his fierce anger rose
And wheeling the strong steeds he rode her down
Until her little limbs beneath the hoofs
Were crushed like willow wands; until the wheels
Across her breast went crackling as the flail
Breaks the low sheaf upon the threshing floor.
And we have laid her by thy mother's grave
Heaping the earth above her, but her blood
Is crying from the wayside dust ye trod
But yestereven. Then the Roman's name
They spake in whispers, but they threatened naught.
For he was great and in his iron hand
Lay life and death for them.

                        The grave new-mad
I sought and in the sunshine smiting down,
Of the dark seeds the dusky woman gave
I planted now another. Many times
From the deep spring I bore the water jar

And poured upon it that its blade might rise
In after days to mark the burial place.
Then, wearied with the lapse of sleepless hours
And the long journey and my anxious toil,
I sought the shelter of a dwarfèd oak
And sank to troubled sleep. Within my sleep
As if through mists unfolded, came the sight
Of level meadows, low and interspaced
With winding still lagoons. And here and there
Upon the trodden fields war horses writhed
Pierced by hard driven arrows. All around
The dead men lay with armor on their breasts.
And nearest of them all, with helmet doffed,
With broken scimetar in his right hand,
Lay my proud father's form, his sable beard
Strown damp upon his corselet. Then the mists
Were inward rolled again and I awoke.
Awoke and said: The dim and slender trust
I had that I might see him ere he died·
Is gone. And all I loved are gone from me.

Then ere the moisture from the grave was dried
That I had watered ere my sleep began,
I digged beside it till the mellowed earth
Was ready for my purpose. Here I laid
The last of the three seeds the woman gave,
And watered it anon, and came away.

In Hebron dwelt a man, Ben Aiden called.
And he was hale though threescore years he bore.
Though silver threads were heavy in his hair
His eye was kindly and his manner free.
He scoffed at Pharisee, and no Essene
Dared measure words with him. For he was learned
In lore of all the Rabbis, and he knew
The pagan scrolls that came from distant lands,
That great Jehovah left in outer dark.
And far Ben Aiden's name was known. His flocks
Grazed many a hillside and his herdsmen raised
Their woolen tents on many a pasture plain.
I sought the village when my task was done

Beside the double graves.   A high dispute
Had risen in the crowd.

By insult stung
A laborer rose and cursed a Sadducee,
Ben Aiden's neighbor.   When thy bones are dust,
He said, Thy spirit in the dark shall lie
Vexed by infernal fire.   Thy deeds shall rise
On thy seared sight.   For senses thou shalt have
To suffer, though thy flesh be passed away
In noisome odors and to clay more foul.
And thine own scorn shall mock thee, and thy pride
Shall be a dungeon for thee evermore;
While we, the toilers, from thy iron hand
Released, shall bask in everlasting peace.
Aye!   Go thy way, he said, beneath thy blows,
Weakened by hunger and by grief distraught,
Because of thy fierce anger I shall go,
And thou wilt bide awhile when I am gone.

Yet we will meet again. I wait for thee.
Yea. At God's Judgment Day, I wait for thee.

With trembling lips and arm flung high he turned
And disappeared. Then loud Ben Aiden laughed;
The beggar, quoth he, sings the ancient song
And through his nostrils makes the old complaint.
Then noting how the list'ners shrank to hear
The fearsome words the angered man had said
He took a softer tone.

    The dream is fond
But futile as the idle wind that blows
And wastes itself afar. Not Abraham,
Or Isaac, or yet Jacob told the myth;
For they were wise. But when our fathers bowed
Beneath the willows of far Babylon,
Eating the bitter bread of banishment,
They from their fellow-slaves within the land
Learned thus to dream. And when they came again

To this their heritage they knew no more
The simple truth the olden prophet taught,
He shall come up no more, who goeth down
Into the silent tomb. But life is sweet
To him who rails not like yon wrathsome wretch,
But loves it day by day and feedeth it
With tribute of the senses in their time.
Ye know that I, Ben Aiden, am no fool.
And ken that I am rich. Ye know, my son
Is favored by King Herod in his pomp.
'Mong all of Israel's daughters, who more fair
Than she who calls me father. In my face
Ye see of health abounding. And mine arm
Is strong at threescore. Who more blest than I
Within our Hebron's borders? More than this,
A few days hence I seek Jerusalem
That I may higher rise: my voice be heard
In Councils of the King. Yet through my years
I've scorned this thought of judgment and of life
Beyond the burial place. Yea, spat upon

The very altar stones; yea, since my youth,
Full forty years agone, defied the God
Ye call Jehovah. And I prosper still.
And ye, my neighbors, love me for my ways,
My bluff plain speech, my gifts of wine and oil
In days of famine.

     With his arms outspread,
And sparkling eye and pleasant boastful voice
He charmed the crowd. And I among the rest
Admired his mien of valor. Then my gaze
He caught with jovial glance. Aye, lad, he said,
Why wilt thou mourn when mourning ever fails;
Or lean on broken reeds of foolish faith.
Ye know the fields where, called of Chalcedon,
The drooping lilies blossom and their scent
Is heavy on the air. They rise, they bloom,
They fade and wither and, anon, are gone,
And others in their places come anew.
Cans't thou the perfume of the yester year

Gather again for petals dropped and dead.
When this thou doest, bring the spirit fond
Back to the eyes that once were bright to thee.

Heartsick, I faltered. Seeing me aghast,
For he was kindly in his boist'rous heart,
I meant no harm, he said, but know the truth
And face the stormy day that soon may turn
To warmth of fav'ring sunshine. Come with me.
I am thy friend and will thee counsel give
As I myself have followed. All is vain
That prates of life beyond this pleasant earth;
And vainer still the prattle that doth say
Thou shalt deny the pleasure of thy days.
Thy labor lighten with deep draughts of wine.
And in thy rest be joyous with the sound
The straken timbrel gives. For we shall die
And all be ended then. Again he laughed,
With his broad hand laid gently on my head.
Yet seeing me despondent, spake again.

Aye, merry be, but yet if wrath do come
Smite hard thy foeman that his fear may be
A tribute to thy strength in hearts of men,
And thou be glorified. An eye for eye,
Yea, tooth for tooth require. So Moses writ,
And blood for blood. So I, Ben Aiden, add.
He was so strong his hand a shelter seemed.
His words were wisdom to me for I knew
Men called him wise and great; and being kind
In word and tone, he seemed a friend to me.
So when he said, come with me, I will make
Thine heart rejoice within the hour, I went;
And with him joined the feast where wine was
    flown
In crystal beakers, and where viands spread
As I had never known; where dancing girls,
In silken raiment, from far Egypt brought,
Wrought sensuous grace of movement in our sight.
Anear the midnight when the nutty fumes
With stupor overcome me, for a jest

They bore me to the vineyard. In the press
They laid me on the pomace. At the dawn,
With laughter loud they sought me and their mirth
Was praise to me. They said that like a man
I grasped the goblet filled with mellow wine.
But yestermorn beneath the temple roof
I saw the holy ark, and seven branched
The golden candlestick shed lambent light
Upon the altar. And my fervent heart
Was awed and hallowed. Now, an hundred years
Seemed passed since then.

     As in an archer's hand
A bow may break and so be thrown away,
My faith of yesterday was failed and gone
Into the common wrack of useless things
Forgotten and forlorn. No more I cared
To mark the varied glory of the skies
Or hues within the wild flowers dainty breast.
The bird-note carolled from the coppiced glens,

Or kraken from the grain, was idle sound
Waking no chord responsive. In the wheat
I saw the thin spires dwindle 'mid the tares
And said, each liveth for itself alone,
The greater strength doth conquer. From the hills
I saw the eagle from his high nest drift
On steady sloping wings and from the fold
Snatch the weak lamb and lordly soar again,
Whereon I said. The innocent shall die
And strength shall conquer still.

    So triple years
Deepened in me the change, and I grew strong;
Foremost in labor—yet the first to hear
The jangle of the cymbal when the day
Gave way to mirth of even. More than all:
The readiest to meet the wrestler's skill,
Or share in festivals the rivalry
With warrior's shaft and blade. I loved the smiles
Of bonny brown-eyed maids. From horn or cup

Or hollowed gourd I drank the brimming wine
In joy or weariness, in rest or toil.
And morn and noon and night each guerdon gave
To my full senses and my bounding heart.
For morn had freshness of the dawn and brought
Brave thoughts of triumph in the daily toil.
And noon of languid rest within the shade
With free songs sung and careless stories told.
And eve the pleasaunce of dark eyes that shone
With light reflected from mine ardent gaze;
And voices breathing music to the sound
Of tinkling instruments that gave us mirth
In steady measure of the graceful dance.

'Twas long ago. Strong-armed and fleet of limb,
I climbed the beetling cliffs, and, falcon-eyed,
Beheld afar the rugged waters flow
In glittering foam through gorges of the hills.
And where the fountains shone beneath the moon
I wooed the maidens from the village strayed.

Oft in the golden vintage drank the must,
Joyous that life was sweet and strength was mine.
Often I hurled the slender javelin
As never Roman threw it. And the shaft
Of Parthian archer never from the bow
Clove the air farther than mine arrows flew.
I joyed in strength as strong men know of joy,
As earth rejoices in the glow of sun,
Or cedars rise exultant in the storm.

Yea, strong I was. And oft the Roman's name
Was coupled in my heart with wrathful thought
Of all his evil deed. I waited long
To hear that he to Hebron came again,
Or drove his chariot on the lonely roads
Among the winding vales. At last he came,
And passed me scornful as I wrought my task
Alone within the field. The steeds were strong;
But I was mightier, and with heavy grasp
I flung them on their haunches. Quick he sprang,

Short sword in hand. But with deft wrist I turned
The blade aside. My hand upon his throat,
A crimson flood from out his nostrils swept.
I dashed him down upon the rocks that lay
Below the wayside ledge, and he was still.
In distant lanes the furious horses reeled,
Dragging the chariot's broken shaft between:
And far through all the country went the tale
How his wild coursers slew him.

                                        In my joy
I drank anew the fervor of the vine,
Welcomed the dalliance of the maidens fond,
And bore a secret triumph in my heart.

Aye, that was long ago. There came a morn
When, from the wassail of the vintage night,
I went afield and through the darkness passed
With reckless shout and song; and lo! mine arm
Was like a spear shaft broken or a blade

Wherefrom the hilt hath dropt. And all my strength
Was vanished into fear until the dawn
And light and warmth came to me, and I rose
With wondering sadness; and bethought me how
The pool was troubled, and that healing came
To those who sought its waters at the morn.
Then all my haughty spirit rose again
As I pressed forward, though my wither'd arm
Hung helpless as I strode.

                The herbage swayed
Beside my rapid steps until the dew
Fell glistening on my feet. The air was still,
Yet seemed a breeze before me, in my face
Blown silently and cool. Anon, I saw
The sombre arches and the gleaming pool
And waiting people there.

                A crippled youth,
With sinews scorched by fire what time a roof

Fell flaming on his bed, was in my way,
And I with lusty shoulder threw him by.
A widow, old and palsied, moaning crept
Across my path; and I, with sturdy laugh,
Stepped over and across. And by the brink
A blind man sat, with wavering hands out-thrust
To feel when first the waters should be stirred;
And at his cry I saw a ripple drift
Across the pool, and sprang beyond him far
Until the healing wave surged on my breast.
Whole I departed, and with buoyant step
I sought anew the fountain and the vine.

For life was sweet, and strength was joy to me,
And rapid moons went by and earth was fair;
I saw the white flowers of the olive fall
As winds swept by them: and beheld the grapes
Turn dusk and golden on the sunny slopes.
I watched the shadows sleep beneath the oaks
That crowned the hills; and the low hyssop grow

Along the curb around the well where shone
The stars reflected in the summer eve;
And where the maidens came, and castanets
Made joyous music for our wanton feet.

Anon, the must was trodden in the vats,
The first ripe olives fell, the thistle raised
Its head above the grain.   And once again
The vintage days were come.

    Aye, long ago
It was that from the dance, with wine o'erwrought
Once more I went afield ere yet the dawn
Touched the tall date tree with its purple ray,
And wandered where the brambles, wet with dew,
Clogged my weak feet.

     In dreamless sleep I lay
Until the high sun smote me, and I sought
To go my way.   But like a bow unstrung

Were all my limbs: and sudden, wond'ring fear
Made my heart faint.   Nor did I move nor rise
Or more than cry along the vacant path
Till travelers, for plenteous gift of gold,
On stout arms bore me as I bid them haste
Far to the pool whose blesséd waters heal
Who first shall touch them as they troubled flow.

There, by the porches five, a little while
They laid me down.   The crippled youth forebore
To pass beyond.   The widow, old and wan,
Spread her scant raiment on my naked feet,
And he who, blinded, held his trembling palms
To feel the waters quiver, stepped aside,
With patient air as more than sight had laid
On him a charge of pity.   Yet, I laughed
As strong arms bore me o'er their heads and laid
Me down amid the waters as they surged
And o'er me swelled with healing in their touch.

So. Whole I rose, and whole I went away.
I careless trod the path that led afar
To famed Engedi's vineyards. Yet the air
Seemed sultrier than before; the way more steep;
The wild birds' song more distant; and the leaf
That from the olive drooped had duller grown.
Upon my tongue the wine found meaner zest,
And the pomegranites juice was cool no more.
The resonant timbrel that a wayward girl
Struck with free fingers as she glanced aside
Had undertone of sadness; and the laugh
That kindled her dark eyes was vain to me.
I lay a while beneath a zaccum branch,
And saw the hot noon waver 'gainst the sky
Till sleep came o'er me; and the lambent stars
Looked down ere I from restless dreams awoke
To dreamy wakefulness and discontent.

I thought. In Hebron have my years been passed.
And there their days monotonous and slow

Pass on from eve to eve. I would the change
Of unknown faces and new pleasures came
To rouse my listless senses. I have heard
That far Engedi hath a fount more broad,
With cooler waters, and upon the wall
The hyssop greener clings. That her ripe grapes
Grow larger clusters, and her wine more bright
Flows than from Hebron's presses. That her maids
Their rounded arms fling wide with grace more free,
And softer sing the canticles of love.

In fair Engedi found I welcome warm,
For they had heard of Shobab bold and blythe,
And glad were they that I had come to them.
There day by day the vintage passed away,
And day by day the seed time slow returned,
When flowers new budded bloomed. And day by
    day
The green grapes turned to purple. Day by day
Soft lute and viol lured me to the fount

When fell the dusk, and pleasant voices spoke
Sweet words of welcome—and the wine was old
And sparkled from the goat skin as it poured.
I craved a draught more potent than the press
Yields from its pomace to the vintner's tread.
Aye.   It was long ago.

     There came an eve:—
The upper vat was heapéd high with grapes,
While that below with wine o'er ran its rim.
They said: Let us rejoice and drink the must,
And drink the old wine, too, for life is sweet.
Then let the tabor and the timbrel sound;
For joyousness is life.   And let us dance.
Aye.   Man and maiden dance.   Soft night is here
And who hath seen to-morrow.   And the morn
Our wassail saw ere yet it touched the east.
But when the last star withered from the sky,
Each gaily homeward turned.   One down the vale,
Another o'er the hill crest, and beyond

The winding stream another. Here and yon
Each one departed gaily while the song,
And tinkle of the timbrel, answered back
One to another till a silence came;
And I alone remained beside the well
Where crept the hyssop on the curb and where
The gourd half filled beside the wine skin lay.
Alone I stood, and all the air was pale
And dulled the glamour of the rosy dawn.
I stooped and from the gourd I drank again
And sang a husky song. Aye, life is sweet
With love and wine and joyaunce of the lute,
I sang, and sang again, till on my brain
There fell a cloud, and all my limbs were like
The aspen's leaves that shiver in the noon
When no breeze stirs the bough.

                The morning air
Was full of golden motes that sank and swam
Before my dizzy sight. A veil of mist

Fell gray upon mine eyes, then sudden dark.
Unto mine ear, like murmuring of bees,
Slow droning sounds from out the silence came.
Prone to the earth I fell, nor anymore
Did sound or sight come to me 'till I woke
From out a dreamless torpor when the dew
Lay sweet and heavy on the mountain grass,
And the white moonlight shone upon a palm
That feathery shadows threw along the way.
I was athirst, and from the herbage lapt
The dripping dew. Ahungered, I beheld
Ripe dates drop, one by one, from out the palm
A dozen: and from one to one I crept
And gathered greedily.

              Then, with bowed head,
With drooping shoulders, and with limbs that shook
As shake the aspen leaves when storms are nigh,
I travailled t'ward the city. Aye. The pool,
The pool, I cried, whose turbid waters quake

In healing turbulence.   The trailing moon
Sank in its radiance from the azure deep.
The cold night wind grew colder and the light
Of the clear stars changed slowly into dawn
Ere I beheld the city, yet afar
Ten thousand cubits.   All the eastern sky
Grew crimson and then faded into blue—
The while the sunshine deepened.   Piteously
I kept upon my way.   The noon was past
And sultriness was slumbering in the vales
Ere low by Kedron's bank I lay my head.
Nor farther wrought for wretchedness and woe,
Or uttered any cry for very pain
And weary hopelessness.

    Here while I lay
I heard the voice of wailing drawing near
And saw along the valley slowly wend,
To where the children of the people lie,
With dubious step a tattered cavalcade.

And as they neared I saw Ben Aiden's son
With wine-flushed face reel where the mourners led,
I heard their voices speak Ben Aiden's name;
And there Ben Aiden's daughter raised her eyes
With sensual glance nor even grief could slake
Of all its coarse alluring. Deeper fell
My heart in loneliness and misery,
For I had known him in the lusty days
Of all my earliest youth, and I had thought
He would befriend me in Jerusalem.

Then merciful a deep forgetful sleep
Weighed softly on mine eyes. The ardent sun
Crept through my limbs, a little comforting;
And blown from Olivet came scent of flowers,
The rustle of high branches and the song
Of birds rejoicing in the peaceful day.
A pleasant dream came to me: rhythmic words
By maidens sung beneath the summer sky:
And jangle of clear cymbals. And I woke

To the sweet voice of women, on the air
Breathed gay and dulcet; and the clang of arms
Like cymbals jangling or like castanets
By wild free fingers struck.

Behold! The King,
The mighty Herod with a train of spears
And shields and glitt'ring corselets. Mid the throng
Of clanging horsemen came the silken dames
In carven chariots riding. On it swept,
Nor would have noted, had a restless steed
Not broken suddenly and sprang aside
And reared and sprang again. A lazar here!
A captain cried, and vengeful swung aloft
His blade as if to smite me; but the king
Saw mark for bitter jest. He bade them bear
Me o'er the brook and to the porches five.
Perchance, he said, the wave may make him clean;
Then at the miracle shall wonder rise;
Aye, we shall marvel much.

His myrmidons
The while the throng passed onward bore me up
And carried me within the city gates, and then,
Their master out of sight, beside a wall
Flung me down rudely and with scoff and jibe,
Left me alone. Then drowsily anew
I felt the creeping heat. I dreamed of feasts
And of cool draughts of water and of wine
Crushed from new ripened clusters, and anon
I restless woke. Ahungered and athirst
My moan I made and no man hearkened me.
Slow, cubit after cubit, through the night
I crept the city streets.

Before the dawn,
Among the earliest who trod the way,
I reached the pool, and with my hollowed hand
Lifted its turbid waters to my lips,
And as one famished, drank; the while a wound
That in my arm a jagged stone had made

Upon its edge dropped blood.   Then from her
    robe—
Yea, scant and thin it was—the widow tore
A bandage narrow, and the hurt she bound
With tremulous fingers and with pitying words
In aged quaver spoken.   He whose limbs
Were scored and seamed by fire gazed curiously,
Deep in my hungry eyes, and from his breast—
His only bread for all the livelong day—
Drew forth of carob pods and gave to me.

The slanting sun shone on the pavement stones,
A green branch waved across the arch where clear
The blue sky met the eye.   A spider's thread
Its venomed burden swayed beside the wall;
And clear a linnet's song swam high above
The clamor of the street.   For now the tread
Of hurrying crowds grew loud.   The bubbles rose
And broke upon the pool.   A sullen wave
Rolled from its centre to its verge, and then

Above us, sandaled or unshod, the feet
Of all the rabble passed. Flung far aside,
And trampled on, we lay—the weak—while all
Those lesser maimed and ill sprang rudely on.
One, with some little ailment, touched the wave
And buoyant and rejoicing went his way.
Then each departed, some with murm'ring words,
Some hopeful of the morrow. All save we
To whom a home and archway were the same;
For us the sun was something in the morn,
The shade a guerdon in the noon, and eve
When all the stones grew cold, alone of all
The hours would drive us forth with willingness.

So day by day nor any change was wrought,
Or any kind vicissitude of woe.
Each morn the waters stirred, each morn the strong
Received its blessedness, each morn the weak
Fell helpless 'neath their strength; and so, at last
We sought, devoid of hope, though seeking still.

'Twas long ago—yea, very many years
Since first I brake the carob by the pool,
And one year like another, save a change,
Impalpable and slow, of which we recked
Or cared nor jot or tittle. We who found
Companionship that morn, a common bond
Of suffering made and waiting, each for each,
Gave greeting when we met. For yet alone
Hath no man stood, nor any burden borne
Unaided by his fellows. In the dawn
Ere yet the sun arose the blind man reached
His hand to feel the waters. In the dawn
The widow's eye grew keen to watch the pool;
And in the dawn the crippled youth crept near
Its edge to be the first, and I, again
Expectant, but unhoping, watched the drift
Of stray leaves on its surface. Then the crush
And struggle of a moment and the sound
Of fast receding feet; while slow and calm
The waters sank anew to placidness,

And drowsy from the tumult silence came.
Then we, upon the scanty alms that fell
To us from careless givers, broke our fast;

We watched on all the things that came and went
Within our little sphere. The swallow's flight
Or high or low, foretold the sun or storm.
The beetle creeping from the creviced stones
Was herald of the dilatory Spring
And scant or heavy harvest, while the fly,
As late or early, forecast for the hills
The yield of spotted melons. And the mouse
As he was sleek or gaunt, the promise gave
Of olive laden boughs or barren branch.
Yea, when the wind veered from the chilly east
We counted that men's hearts would kindlier be
Upon the morrow. When from out the west
The wind blew fair and steadfast, well we knew
That from the seacoast marts the millet cakes

Would cheapened come. And when from the far
    south
It slowly blew and steady, sure, we said
The dancing girls will seek the porches five
And we shall hear the cymbals and the song.
Whene'er the vapor on the gray cold walls
Gathered in drops and slowly trickled down,
The plague, we said, will devastate the land,
And prayed for each who in the morning gave
To us our daily pittance. When afar
The thin clouds sailed across the azure skies,
And leaves turned sidelong as the wind went by,
Behold, we said, the thunder and the rain
Shall stay the pestilence, and we shall hear
The chanting of the priests in thanks to God.

Aye, more than this, we watched the black ants
    climb
By devious pathways to the coping stone
That crowned the arch, and heavy laden bring

The gummy residue from leaves that swept
Against the outer pillars, lo, we said,
How gain doth come from patience. Oft we saw
The driving swallows in their reckless flight
Dash headlong 'gainst the wall and, fallen low,
Lie motionless as dead, 'til breath of breeze
And blessedness of sun slow brought them back
To joyous flight again. Then comforting
Ourselves with gentle thoughts, 'tis thus, we
        cried,
The Father's hand shall lift us into peace
And healthfulness of days. When, oftentimes,
The outland camels choked the narrow streets
Until the rich man's litter could not pass,
Nor Levite keep the path; and when the steed,
Caparisoned for war, raised hoof in vain:
The Gibeonite with water jar on head
Thridded between, and singing went his way.
So shall we pass, we whispered, when the great
Are stayed and humbled.

Yea, more than this.
From out the legends of a billowy past,
Where truth shone for a moment and was gone,
We gained quaint stories that would comfort us.
As of one, leprous stained, who painful drew
From plains beyond the Jordan, and while night
Still mantled all the earth, lay down and slept
A weary sleep beside the blesséd pool:
Yet dreaming, when the sunlight smote his face
With its first beam; gave vigorous stroke and fell,
Ere yet the strongest sprang, and in the wave
Left all his leper's whiteness and was clean.
And of one, cunning, who in distant woods
A curious fabric made of springing branch
And intertwining leaf, and hid therein,
Close by the marge, so that the pilgrims thought
A bunch of wild acacias lay anear
The edges of the water, 'til he flung
Himself abroad when first the ripples stirred,
And reached them earliest and himself was healed.

Nor lacked we laughter, sad and slender mirth
Was ours in many a languid afternoon
When olden jests retold gave hollow cheer:
Or for an hour a new freak pleasaunce gave,
Thus, where pomegranate skins were flung beside
The portals of the arches, came the flies
In darkening clusters, and the crippled youth
Would deftly catch them and with pride would show
The buzzing captives; and sometimes a bee,
White faced and droning in its drowsy flight,
Would fearless clasp. And so it happed, one day,
An alien wasp by favoring winds far blown,
Drifted within the gates; with agile hand
He grasped it as it sped and quick was stung,
Whereat we laughed, full long; and many a day
The jest made light the languor of the hours.

There came ofttimes, a fair and pleasant youth
Who studied with the priests, that he might speak
Some day in the Sanhedrim. He was kind

And told us stories of the ages gone
Unwritten in the scrolls. And so one day
With mimic manner, as himself were king
Or seer, or beggar, he the story told
How evil Ashmedai, the Amulet
Stole from King Solomon, so he was cast
Into deep sorrow and to Kedesh came
Low wailing in his woe.

    'Twas thus the lad
With varying accent told the legend old:

I, Solomon, the wand'rer, I was King
Over all Israel, in Jerusalem.
Yet now I crave your alms, a beggar's dole
Will blunt my hunger and my need assuage.

Yea, I was Solomon, of Israel King,
And through these streets with horses silver-shod
Rode on in triumph while my chariot wheels
In golden splendor the high sun outshone.

Now I am girt with straw, and on my breast
A tent cloth's fragment shields me from the blast.
So give me alms.

    Yea, Solomon the Great,
Men called me in those days. My sceptre swayed
From Euphrates to Tyre. My stately ships
Were favored of the skies; and Ophir knew
Their white sails swimming on the distant seas.
My bowmen and my spearmen in array
Were mightier than Egypt's mighty hosts
And owned me lord and ruler. Now, the husks
From desert branches are sweet food to me,
Gathered with trembling hands by barren ways.
So give me alms. For it was writ of old
The poor and yet the stranger shalt thou aid
As this our Israel was from bondage brought.

I had the love of women. From afar
Sheba's fond Queen came to my strong embrace.

And who were fairest of the varied lands
Were willing conquest of my ardent heart.
Love songs I sung, and softly kindled eyes
Replied in silence. Now, great Solomon
Wanders unknown. Beyond the eastern gate
One with bronz'd forehead mocked me. Give me alms
For I am faint with travail and with pain:
My eyes are dim and the rough way is dark,
And Solomon would rest a little while
Ere the new day new trouble brings to him.

I owned the charm that demons feared, and knew
The secrets of the genii in their guile.
And innocent craft of fairies and of elves
That haunt the forest dells. Now, demons scoff
At my lost amulet. The genii mock,
And elf and fairy when my feet draw near
Hide in the woodland hollows. I am changed.
Yea, Solomon is changed and all is gone
Save want and woe and bitter barren years

That crave thy pity and thy scanty alms,
For Solomon is weary.   He is weak;
And patient in his asking, for he knows
The poor speak often ere they find reply.

Of God's own Temple the high walls I built,
Nor sound of hammer fell upon the air,
While stone on stone uprose.   The Lord our God
Gave me of wisdom for all holy things,
And knowledge of his work in earth and air
From Lebanon's high cedar to the herb
That sways neglected on the toppling wall:
And vision clear for judgment.   Now, my thought
Heeds but the present hour, and dole that comes
From hearts grown pitiful to see my woe:
For Solomon is broken and his state
Is vanished into rags.   Yea, give me alms.
Me, who was Ruler in Jerusalem,
And Seer.   And priest before the holy Lord.
I, Solomon, the Preacher.   I was King

Over all Israel. Yet my hunger sore
Craves pittance from thee, and I fain would find
Some little shelter from the winds that blow
Through the chill shadows of the creeping night.

I through the cities of this realm have passed,
A stranger 'mid my people, and no door
Swung on its hinges for the king unthroned.
And in the narrow lanes where beggars hide
I found each had his place but none for me.
Amid the graves beyond the outer walls
I sought where I might shelter. But the dogs,
According to their strength, each knew the bound
And limit where he slept, where none might come.
In autumn fields the little fieldmouse sought
His home beneath the stones. The swallow's wing
Swept confident to where below the eaves
His clay-built dwelling hung. The eagle's flight
Grew smooth and sloping when from upper sky
He saw his wild nest resting on the crags.

And I their comfort envied as I walked
Crying with tears: Oh, Israel, I was King
When from Araunah's floor the temple rose,
And David's son ruled in Jerusalem,
Until at last, with sorrow overborne
I ask thine alms.

    Then quoth a fisherman:
Lo! I am poor. No spreading net is mine
As wealthy fishers use. On sturdy feet
I tread the long leagues to far Galilee
Whose waters, like the bounty of the Lord,
Are free to all who come. A slender line
Braided from nettles in waste places grown
Suffices for my need. Within the deep
The fishes come and go; nor do I ken
Or whence or whither. Scant unto my hand
Each day these many years enough has come
To find me food and raiment. Share with me
The solitary bream mine hook hath caught:

And share my fire the while the outer dark
Shall grow forgotten though the chill winds blow:
And with me share my shelter 'til the morn
Shall warmth of sunshine bring to us again.

They sat, the twain, and watched the embers glow
Within a narrow brazier, and the cloud
Of vapor rise the while the food prepared.
And the King's eye grew brighter as he gazed,
His nostrils dilate as the odor rose
From the quick seething flesh. Anon, they ate;
As brothers friendly, though their converse brief.
And when 'twas finished; we are satisfied,
Spake they together, though it all be gone
Save yonder entrails thrown beside the knife
That scored them from their place. But while they
         spake
From out the heap revolting shone a light
Misty and dim and wavering and strange,

As if a gleam of gold and gems were mixt
And overlaid with sulphur's sapphire flame.

Then with a cry, as one o'erwrought with joy,
Sprang Solomon and grasped with trembling hand
The amulet and on his finger placed
Its graven coil.   Then through his raiment rude
Shone all of Kingly manner and of grace:
And power was on his forehead.   In his limbs
The strength of youth was sudden manifest,
But in his eyes was tearful tenderness,
And his red lips were tremulous as are
A mother's words when murm'ring of the dead.

And when the fisherman would kneel to him,
He said, not so, my brother.   Go with me
When comes the morning.   Let us seek the hill
Whence we may Hermon see, and Libanus,
Carmel and Tabor and Esdraelon,
And Galilee's fair valley and her sea

Wherein thy line was dropt.   And tread its shore
Where Sons of God shall travail when my name
Is but a legend in the hearts of men.

They slept.   And when the morning came, he spake:
I, Solomon, The Wand'rer, I am King,
Over all Israel, and Jerusalem
Is mine own city.   Yet mine heart is sad.
For wiser now than when my wisdom waked
The wonder of the nations, I am fain
That all were finished.

     Mine own heart hath known
The weariness and burden of the poor.
And earthliness of sin that bows the weak
Ere they can rise to cry upon the Lord.
The sore temptation; and the bitter fruit
Which follows evil sowing.   Yea.   The thought
That God is far away and will not hear.
And the deep brooding, that the Lord is just,

That we are evil, and his wrath will come
Until his broken law be all avenged.
Not mine the strength or mine the light to know
Wherefore shall mercy come. My spirit faints,
For all is vanity that I have done.
Yet seer am I.

    And now the curtain lifts,
Before the front of Ages vast and dim.
And One shall come, more wise than Solomon,
Purer than Moses, stronger than the sire
Of our proud race. And Him the Lord shall own,
And in Him kindreds of the earth be blest.
Wherein I, Solomon, the weak, am bent,
He shall arise in triumph. Then the poor
By Him shall pass to joy and blessedness.

Then forth they went, the twain, the level sun
Threw thin, long shadows slanting on the path,
Upon the hill where now is Nazareth.

They sought the strand and idle at their feet
The waters lapped with murmurs soft and low,
And the King's face was peace. A placid light
Lay in his eyes; a look as one who turns
From arid pathways into meadows cool;
Or who from battle coming, sees the roof
Of his own dwelling in the restful vale.
His beard the sweet wind wafted, and his hair
From silver threads threw back the mellow sun.
And on his white hand shone the amulet
A wavering drop of gentle sapphire flame.

He said: My brother. Thou wast kind to me
When I was hungered. When I sought for rest
Thy couch gave me the blessedness of sleep.
And I am King and Seer; and spirits own
My power on earth and sea. So, nevermore
In Galilee thy line be vainly cast.
And never shall thy brazier fail of fire.
Nor ever storm assail thee, till ye die

Of many gathered years and kindly age.
The fisher heard and cast his line abroad,
But scarce the sinker fell beneath the wave
Ere the cord tightened. Thrice he drew to land
The finny spoil until it seemed too great
For his strong arms to bear. Then reverently
Obedient to a sign, departed thence.

But in a little while he turned and saw
The Kingly form, the sunlight on its head,
Silent and calm. Then slow the fingers drew
Forth from its place the lambent amulet,
And flung it forth, a gleaming arc in air
That fell and vanished in the midmost sea.
And calm and silent with slow waving beard,
With sunlight on his forehead and his hair,
The King stood on the shore. The fisher saw
And awe was in his heart: and wondering
He turned and went his way. And not again
In this our land was seen great Solomon.

He ceased the tale, half bashful and half pleased
To hear our praises of his mien and speech.
But with his kind good eve the story failed
And faded from our thought. Nor did I dream
I should remember in the after time.

Sometimes a stranger gave us passing cheer.
Once, wandering from the coast a sailor came,
Reckless in word but with a kindly heart,
And gladdened us with alms and willing speech,
For well he liked a list'ner, and we loved
To hear his tales of wondrous lands remote
From all our warriors knew or sages told.

Once, so he said, beyond where Roman spears
Outshone the glimmer of the Northern seas,
He climbed a mountain on whose naked crest
The sunlight lay when deep the midnight brought
Its darkness to the silent lands below.
Yea, there, he said, he saw the sun descend

Aslant and crimson and then rise again,
Yet never sink beneath the distant edge
Of the far driven sea ; and so its course
Kept onward with no twilight and no night,
But ever living radiance on the sky,
And light unbroken on the mountain top.
Then, ever eager to explain her thought,
The aged woman spake. Above the vales
Wherein we dwell the peace of God doth lie
As on the northern summit dwells the sun.
There fear is gone, as on the distant height
The darkness hath no place. Yea, we may climb
From out these lowly shadows into light.

The sailor, hearing, wondered, and gave voice
To long, low, doubting whistle and away
Went with a mocking laugh, forsaking us
As all too simple for his courtesy.

We heard the daily gossip, that which ran
From lip to lip among the folk, and we
Were glad to join therein, because it gave
Us lot and share with human kind around
And made us one with them: we heard and told,
Of who was wed and who was borne beyond
The city gates for burial; and who
Had come into the world; and who was old
And wise, or foolish, and whose wealth was gone,
Or poverty was done; who from afar
Had home returned, or who departed thence.
Sometimes its sluggish current faster moved
At some strange thing new told.

    One early morn,
Yea, it was long ago, but not more clear
Is yesterday within my vision drawn,
Where comes the road from Bethlehem we saw
A wayworn woman hasten to the mart
Where sheep are sold, beyond the healing pool,

And in her arms an infant. Quick she drew,
With trembling fingers and averted gaze,
The coarse, dry herbage from the mangers full
Wherein she wrapped the child, and hiding it,
Sped t'ward the ford of Kedron. Soon we heard
A murmur of shrill voices in the air,
And sobbing near at hand. The Edomite,
They cried, hath slain the innocents and now
Is Rama mourning for her little ones,
Aye, thrice accursed shall cruel Herod be.

And once we heard how from the Eastern lands
A lambent star, new risen, passed athwart
The calm, blue sky, and wise men followed it,
Yea, Kings were they and bore of precious gifts,
Until it paused above a humble roof
Beneath whose shelter oxen chewed the cud
And sheep contented lay. And more they told,
Some doubting much and some of fervent faith.
How in the manger was a new-born child,

Foretold of old a conqueror, and whom
A virgin nursed in purity undimmed
By any guile or stain, and at whose feet
With low obeisance the gifts were laid.

And later still they said this self-same babe
Borne into far-off Egypt safely dwelt,
Awaiting that His time of power should come
When he should rule—a King. The story told,
We pondered for an hour and then forgot,
Seeking new wonder in some newer tale.

But chiefest of the pleasaunce that we knew
That dotted here and there the dismal days
With scattered shards of light—the tales oft told
Of how our people in the olden years
Were God's best chosen. How from Egypt's dark
And crushing bondage all the tribes rose up
With steadfast tread, and sought the purple sea
Whose waters rose beside them, like a wall,

That they might walk dry shod. How smoke and
 flame
Did guide them through the wilderness, and how
The manna fell in darkness of the night
When they were hungered. How beyond the hills
This land allured them, promised of old time,
Where rain from Heaven on the thirsty earth
Should bring forth bread without the touch of foot
To trickling rivulet. How Solomon
These naked streets had clothed with shining gold.
How he had talked with demons and had known
The inmost secrets of the rocks and woods:
And over mighty kings held heavy sway.
How he from Joktan's deserts charmed the queen
That ruled in Sheba. How his daring ships
Of carven shittim wood from seas remote
Brought back of gems, and birds of colors rare.
How, earlier, a shepherd lad had gone
To seek his sheep and found a crown instead.
How, earlier still, when Israel owned the yoke,

A woman drove a tent-pin through the brain
Of the accursed invader. How our sires
Mourned 'neath the willows by the still lagoons
That notched Euphrates' banks. How Esther came
Mantled in beauty to the conqueror,
That by the sword her people yet might live,
Though sorely smitten. How Holofernes
By Judith pure as snow was smote and slain,
And all the people said Amen, and she
Was honored of our God.

                And while we talked
Of these the women of old days, the crone
Her shaking hands held steadier and a light,
Like glint of burnished steel, was in her eyes
The while she crooned. It was a woman's arm
That saved our people in the evil days.
Aye, Israel's maidens are not they who know
Alone fair smiles, and softly woven words
Sweet spoken in the dusk. And more we told

Of many marvels in the ancient days
And told them yet again.

          But most of all
We conned the mystery that Jacob spake
Concerning Judah, that around his hearth
Our race should gather until Shiloh come.
And who, we questioned, shall this Shiloh be,
So long foretold and weary waited for?
The Roman spears are bright along our streets,
And Roman eagles from the standards look
Upon us from our hills. When Shiloh comes,
Shall Judah rise once more ; shall Zion share
Her splendor once again? So queried oft
Our desultory talk when fervently
Each gave interpretation to the tale.
Aye, quoth the greybeard:—

          Judah yet shall know
Her garners filled with harvests and her vales

Ablown with flowers new born. Her ships shall sail
To seas untraversed, as in ancient days,
And all her marts be filled, nor any tread
Of alien warrior in her land be heard.
Not Lebanon with his cedars shall be strong,
Or Sharon with her roses be more fair
Than this our land ; for Shiloh sure shall be
Like unto David, and like Solomon
In all save guile.

     Then answered quick the youth.
Behold, when Shiloh comes, the cymbals' clang
Shall clamor loud from Jordan to the sea,
And all the pastures shall be swept for steeds.
The smiths shall swing the hammers at the forge,
From dawn to dark, that spearheads may be made
To arm the serried hosts. The chariot wheels
Shall grind the pavements of Jerusalem
Rolled outward to the gates. The bronzèd birds
That crown the Roman standards, flown afar

Shall dread our trumpet's blast. Like Joshua,
But sevenfold more than he, shall Shiloh come.

Then softly said the widow, when He comes—
Foretold by prophets, shall a gentle calm
As of a Sabbath morning fall on all.
And wrath shall die and peace be everywhere.
The smiths shall labor, but their cheerful toil
Shall make of ploughshares and of sickles keen
And hooks to till the vines. The trumpet's blast
Shall echo o'er the vales but it shall call
The people to the feasts. The cymbal's sound
Shall have but gladness and the voice of joy.
Yea, in that day the lions from the hills,
The wild men dwelling in the caves, shall come
And seeking peaceful shelter shall lie down
Unharming and unharmed within our walls.
And none shall be ahungered, for the just
Shall say that all God's creatures shall be fed.
And none shall be afraid, for merciful
Shall all men's hearts be found when Shiloh comes.

And I, in reverie, upon the pool
Saw dead leaves dance and shadows come and go.
Once with a step sedate, through summer days
There came a man robust, in gentle guise,
Who spake in voice subdued and gave us alms,
With sympathetic words. Ofttimes he stood
And gazed upon the pool; not when it stirred
In first ebulliance in the rosy light,
But when the shade grew cool at evenfall,
When water spiders darted here and there
Like dots of darker shadow on its face:
When all its deeps grew black and clearer gave
Its dusk reflection to the downward gaze.
There would he ponder long, then with a sigh
Would turn away and bid us soft good-night
As if we were of brotherhood with him.
Whereat we marvelled, for his raiment shone
With linen woven in Cyrenian looms,
And purple gathered from the murex shell.
Upon his hand the cloven diamond shone

Mingled with sapphire and with chrysophrase.
His words were chosen as a Rabbi's are,
Full delicate and dainty in their strength.
And yet he seemed like one of us who knew
The burden of a sorrow held so long
That it was daily use and habitude.
So seeing him we held our woes more light
As of the common burden of the world.
But we knew not his name or whence he came
Till from the fervent heat, one afternoon
A woman sought the arch.

                Beneath the sky
Was never mortal seen more beautiful
In face or form or movement of the limbs,
Or sensuous grace of speech, or tender ways.
Save this, that oft her eyes were sinister,
Nor steadily would gaze into our own:
And that sometimes around her mouth there came
Lines like the leopard's when he nears his prey,

Though seemed she as but yesterday a child.
And her we knew. For we had seen her pass
With flaunting garments, when the twilight came,
And hollow laugh that echoed far and drear.
She, resting, stood within the shade and gazed
Half curiously on us. Her loosened hair,
Like silk from far Sinensis, fleecy fell
A sable cloud unto her languid knee,
And clustered on her forehead low and broad.
She stood, and spake not, till the angered crone
Said, wherefore, woman, comest thou anear:
Thy place is out beyond the utmost gates,
So trouble us no more.

      She answered not;
But with a sudden movement of her arm
Disclosed the rounded bosom and the charm
Of all the ivory shoulder tinged with gold.
And leaned against the wall as leans the vine
Upon the trellis in the noontide heat.

Then with a careless smile said—sweet and soft,
Ah, matron, thou art old: and like the seed
From the ripe thistle blown, art harsh and dry,
And know no juiciness of life, or touch
Of any fervidness of summer noons
On thy cold heart or in thy shrinking veins.
Yea, matron, thou art old and therefore scorn.
I take no coolness from thee in the shade,
Nor crowd thee in the narrow resting place
Beneath this spreading arch. A little while
And I go forth, and leave no word behind
Of bitterness or railing. Let the rose
Bloom forth its little hour. It hinders not
The thistle's seed on chilly winds upborne.

Then spake the blind man. Woman, hearken me,
I listen to thy step and hence I know
That thou art hale and strong. I hear thy voice
And learn thy heart is fond and passionate.
Its buoyant accents tell me thou art fair.

The rustle of thy garments, delicate
Doth hint of sensuous grace and courtesy.
Thy babble is of roses.   Thou can'st see
The splendor of fair fields with blossoms strown.
In all these gifts find ye no treasure lent
For which to make accounting?   Wherefore now
In idle dalliance with the drifting days
Dost loiter far from shelter of the hearth,
And all the peace of home and loving hearts?

Quoth she, and hast thou heard the hammers clang
On anvils of Damascus?   By the doors
Where armorers labored I have marked the scene,
The glitter of the fire and all the roar
And splendor of the forges.   And the steel
Lay ready to the master workman's hand.
And whether from the twisted bar should come
A blade to shimmer on victorious fields
Or one to offer up the sacrifice
Was in his heart alone.   Lo.   He who made

The glory of the sun and earth and skies
Has wrought us to the fashion of his will,
And who shall hinder him.

                             Once knew I truth.
And all the trustfulness of innocence,
Dreaming that love was like the asphodel
That golden grows where gentle spirits are.
When him I met whom ye will see to-day
Beside this pool when evening shadows fall.
For so we twain beside still waters stood,
Beheld our faces in them and the stars
Twinkle below ere yet our tryst was done.
The year hath gone, and sullenly and dark
He sees his own reflected all alone.
And naught save memory of evil done
Hath he and I together. He, who lured
And I, who fell unheeding in the snare.
Yea, I have faltered by the synagogue
To see him, with fond wife, exultantly

Give thanks before the altar of the Lord:
Wearing phylacteries a handbreadth broad,
And mark the smiles that all the people gave,
As in obeisance, did he but deign
To look upon them there. Then have I gone:
And shame has followed me along the streets,
The mocking of the beggar and the jest
Of Levite passing on the other side.
Yea, shame and hunger, and the bitter woe
That comes from dearth of converse with our kind,
And memory of sweet hours forever dead.
Aye, blind man, thou art darker in thine heart
Than in those clouded eyes, to speak of home,
Or hearthstone shelter, or sweet peace to me.

Then, turning, with slow steps she went away.
But in a little while we heard her sing
As if her sorrow a slow comfort found
In self-communing words.

                    Aye, love is sweet.
When love is guiltless, as the rose is fair
Untouched by ardor of the fervid noon.
Ah, Love is life and love is dead to me.
And life were better ended as the rose
Dies in the blaze of suns that gave it birth.
Among the branches darker grew the shade
And deeper all the shadows 'neath the arch,
When at the accustomed hour we heard the step
Of him of whom she spoke; but all our hearts
Had grown a-cold to him. Yet seeing this
He smiled, surprised, and threw a double dole,
Two coins, to each and passed toward the pool,
And spake no more to us. Anon, we heard
Him murmur softly, to himself alone:

Vain are my gifts upon the altar laid
And vain the travail of the stormy years,
The gathering of gold, and praise of men.
Yea, and the love of woman, cast away

Like blossoms brought with toil from rocky cliffs
Then flung upon the wayside when the joy
Hath passed a little space. Aye, vain the faith
Our fathers brought from sore captivity,
That we shall rise from out the sepulchre
To a new Eden. Yet, mayhap, as vain
The Sadduseean's sullen dream of death,
A sleep wherein no visions come to us.
Aye. All is vain. Yet Death the riddle solves.
This calm, still water could the marvel tell
To who would trust it. When the gentle breath
Had bubbled to its surface he would know
The mystery of all the dark beyond.

Drowsy we listened to his monotone
That fell on our dulled senses till it seemed
Receding and confused. Then slumber came
With dreams that flitted in awakening
Ere we could hold them as a pleasure known
Or anguish undergone. For we awoke

To hear shrill cries of wonder and of woe.
For they who sought for him who watched the pool
Need seek no more, and lamentation made.
He lay beneath the water, save that fair
Above its surface shone his forehead high,
And hand bedight with jewels. From the space
Of all the arches swarmed the flies and sank
In clusters on his brow. And still he lay,
For on that morn no angel touched the pool:
And none were healed in presence of the dead.

Then we were filled with sorrow at the thought
Of all our coldness to him. And we told,
In low, remorseful converse, of his gifts
And many kindly words. I safely laid
The two denarii in my girdle's fold,
That I might keep them for his memory's sake
Till need should wrench them from me. Many days
Were flown ere we forgot to think of him
When sunshine faded and the night drew near.

Once, tempted by the coolness of the air
When after rain the sunlight fell subdued,
An hour before the dark, we sought the street;
The blind man guided by our willing hands;
Our weakness holpen by his greater strength,
Till, eastward thrown, the shade of David's tower
Made welcome resting place. And there were come
A-many curious list'ners to the voice
Of one who cried:—

                  Ah, mine inheritance
Hath gone from me. Within the outland vales
A crafty chief made foray where the flocks
Of many poor and lowly, scattered grazed;
And spoiled the fields of harvests where his hand
Had thrown no kernel in the seeding time;
And garnered orchards that old women watched
From flower to fruitage with dim, anxious eyes,
Mocking their tears with many a laughing jest
And scoff at all their pleading. Yet, he thrives,

This Mahu Jael, while he scorns the law.
Yea, while my heritage he harried sore—
And drove me forth alone, still was he blest.
So my inheritance hath passed away
And to my children poverty hath come.

Then spake a Greek, an epicurean called,
Clad in soft raiment but with manner cold.
Why raise thy voice complaining that the stroke
Of Mahu Jael heavy on thee lies.
Match thou his craft with guile, his force with strength,
His plotting with thy patience. Know'st thou not
That men, like vipers, struggle, and the strong,
The wise, the resolute rear head aloft
And hiss, triumphant, while the vanquished lie
Broken and crushed. Go seek thy place afar
From toil and struggle. Mahu Jael's head
Shall fall like thine at last and all be done.
What will it matter. Who will bear the tale

Unto our children's children, or will care
That thou wast spoiled; that Mahu Jael laughed,
Or that I touched thy sorrow with rebuke.

With slow, uneasy thought I heard his words
As if I—half unmeaning—shared their guilt.

Then we the blind man guiding with our sight,
And he our weakness aiding with his arms,
Sought once again our places by the pool
Curtained anew with shadows. But that eve
We were more sad, as if the stars more far
Were drawn within the sky, and hope more faint
Would mingle with the coming of the dawn.

Light fell the snow upon Jerusalem;
'Twas years thereafter, and within the porch,
From out the falling flakes, the loiterers drew,
And with them came the homeless and the weak
Who knew no other shelter. Then I heard

Once more of Mahu Jael. For the Greek,
His face grown older but his eye alert
And manner affable, came with the rest.
He to my query answered, yea, I knew
This Mahu Jael to the day he died.
And ever as of old he scorned the law.
Lived long by the strong hand and strangled fell
By stronger hands than his. A wild wolf's cry
That rose and sank to silence, that is all
Of Mahu Jael in his life and death.

Nay, 'tis not all. So, clear and shrill, a voice
Made answer to the words. He cannot die
Save in the flesh that he hath left behind,
As the brown beetle on the cedar's side
Leaves empty shard when he himself hath passed
Into a life renewed.

    I, list'ning turned
And saw one clad in raiment torn and old,

Of camel's hair close woven. On his beard
Lay lucent drops of honey. In his hand
Were locusts crisped by fire, whereof he ate
The while he said to us.

The merciless

Hath gone to judgment and his doom is wrought
In flame unmerciful through endless days.
And he who justice mocked doth justice know.
For God is just. In all consuming fire
That yet consumes not his keen consciousness,
Are memories like sting of asps to him
Of wrongful purpose and the fruit it bears
On, on, and on, until the world shall end.
And all the good he scoffed unto his thought
Is clear and vivid, and in shadowy forms
Reveals to him the good that might have been,
Had he but willed it, till the world shall end;
And yet was not nor evermore shall be.
For God is just. Yea, every deed shall bear

According to its kind, as 'mid the hills
Each drifting seed hath kindred in its yield
Of more than is itself.

     Then who shall bear,
The Greek replied, the weight of his own sin,
Though he be sorrowful before he dies
That no atonement made he in his day,
And now the time be gone. Aye, who shall pay
Of his own debt of evil at the last.
Repent. Repent, and ye shall have of time,
Replied the prophet. There is One who comes—

But, ere his words were finished, from the street
Came voice of ribaldry and clank of chain,
And a decurion with his followers came.
They seized the prophet. With rude hands they bound
The iron links on unresisting limbs.
King Herod wills, they said, thy rebel heart

Shall break in dungeons by the pitchy sea;
For thou hast spoken ill of one he loves.
Grasping his beard they bore him speedily
Forth from our midst, and him I saw no more.

From seedtime unto harvest steadfastly
The lagging seasons rolled, and one by one
These my companions left me. Intervals
Of years were lain between but I alone
At last remained. Nor any joy was mine,
Through any of the evanescent days,
When they were gone. For alien every face
Saving these three to me. Nor any voice
Other than theirs attuned to friendliness.
Yet in the joyless hours I yet rejoiced
For peace was theirs, and gentleness; and care
Was gone from them afar. For so it was
That all from me went out into the day,
The shadows dusk behind them and the light
On their glad faces. One by one they went

And all my throbbing heart went out with each.
While I was left to watch the shadows play
Upon the eddying water, and the leaves
Float here and yon as soft winds wafted them.

For once there came a morning when the stars
Shone dull and red through all the filmy haze.
As was his wont the blind man on the brink
Sat him a-low with unexpectant trust.
A ruffian from the Arab wilderness,
Swart, strong and lithe as desert tigers are;
Drunken with lees from outcast wineskins drawn,
And wild with all the terror Ishmael knows
Within the walls of cities, frantic sprang
Into our midst. With reckless arm outswung
He smote the sightless watcher that he fell.
And at the instant, lo! the waters swayed
Sweeping the blinded face, caressing it
With softly flowing touch and lapping low
The fallen form with ripples delicate.

He rose and saw the glory of the sun
New born beyond the east. He marked the clouds
Like silver mantles flung upon the sky:
The dim green of the olives, and the shine
Of almond leaves, afar: the shade that wove
A fretwork from the branches where the breeze
Slow swayed them to and fro: then scanned each face
In wonder turned toward him; but he knew
Not us who shared his solitary years
Until we spake with loud rejoicing words,
But with a little envy in our hearts
That shrank ashamed ere it ourselves we knew,
For he was hale as aged men are hale
Who all their days have honor'd God's behests.
And peace was on his forehead and his lips
Were sweet with sympathy for us who lay
Still bounden in the bondage of our woe.
Behold, He said. As dwell one family
Within a peaceful tent in lonely lands,

So underneath the arches have we stayed.
I go not hence but to return again.
A little while I wander where the graves
Of all my people be. A little while
Shall note the strangeness of the hills and mark
How the old paths are changed that thread the vale.
And with awakened sight shall see once more
The changeless wild flowers bloom, as long ago
I saw them in the fields. But on each day
That comes before the sabbath I will come
And we shall speak again our simple words:
Again shall know each other, and the hearts
Of each shall open in all kindliness.
And if it chance I come not, and no word
Before the sabbath hear ye, know that I
Have passed beyond the twilight into day
Whence never voice returneth.

      Then he went
In the new risen sunlight, but each noon

When drew the sabbath near he came to us;
Sometimes with ripened clusters from the vines
Of distant vintage grown, sometimes with dates
Gathered beside the narrow path that led
From the far fountain down; with pomegranates
And figs and carob pods of sweeter taste
Than on the wild trees grew. And roses oft,
With tender lilies from the wayside dells,
And mosses woodland grown. At last a day
Before the sabbath passed nor heard his step
Upon the stones, or saw his shadow cast
Between the pillars. Then we knew that he
Was nevermore for us.

       Then after years
Crept by more slowly still. One leaden morn
When thin clouds veiled the sky and airs were
  cold
Though scarce the wet leaf stirred beside the wall;
We heard the sound of hautbois floating near

In measured cadence, and the shriller tone
Of loud blown dulcimers. The steady tread
That warriors keep beneath a chieftain's eye.
The rattling of the sword on greaves of steel,
And clinking of the mail on jarring shields.

Anon within our sight the gleam of spears,
The orderly array of arméd men,
And in their midst a litter high upborne;
A crimson canopy above, below,
Fair golden tassels trailing, and around
Broad curtains broidered with the strange designs
The women of Euphrates weave and blend.
For now a satrap, from beyond the hills
That mark the utmost limit of our land,
Laid low by poison and anear the grave
Had come to seek for healing in the pool.
When stopped they by the brink we fell away,
Crowded on either hand, and left clear space
For litter and for bearers, while they paused

To wait the troubled waters. But the youth,
A youth no more but with thin scattered threads
Of silver in his beard, more bold than all
Drew close unto the litter till he touched
The drooping tassels, and with smiling face
Made friendship with the soldiers. So he placed
His hands upon the smooth and burnished shields,
And of their inlaid silver traced the course
With curious fingers. And with pleaséd eyes
Noted the inwrought armlet of the chief,
The golden ornaments each cuirass bore,
And the keen spears and crescent cimetars:
The while the hautbois spake more low, and less
Of strident tone came from the dulcimers,
Until they ceased.

     And we were silent all.
So silent that I heard, far overhead,
A little sound as if a bee had thrown
Himself against the ceiling, or a twig

Wind borne had rustled on the sloping roof:
Yet sibilant as if a viper's tongue
On high had darted and then hid again.
Then, downward shot from where the highest arch
Its keystone hid in shadows, fell a stone
Age-loosened from its place.

                Like gossamer
The silken folds that crowned the canopy
Were riven as it fell. Above the head
That lay upon the pillow swung the hand
Unscathed of old by fire. Yea, as it caught
The white-faced bee long since in idle play
Thus now it seized the stone, then cast it down
So that it fell in ripples in the pool.

The Satrap spake. Beyond the mountains far
A hundred thousand people sleep in peace.
And rise in peace at morn, and through each day
In peacefulness pursue the pleasant round

Of life and labor all devoid of fear.
For I in justice rule them.   Long ago,
Ere age had tempered all my fiery blood,
I laid up need of all atonement man
May make unto his fellows.   Thou has gained
For them, of blessèd years, and fair for me
The yet atoning time.

     Behold, He said,
On yon dull water bubbles rise and fail
And glisten in the glamour of the sun.
Then lay me down upon these pavement stones,
Aye, at this cripple's feet, and bear him in
When highest thrown the troubled waters break.
And, as he bade, they laid the litter down,
A burning heap of splendor, where the rays
Threw their new risen light.   Then speedily
They placed the cripple where the waters rose.

He knelt and kissed the graven armlet then,
With grateful streaming eyes, then turned aside

To us his old companions. Nevermore
Be sad, quoth he, for ere the Sabbath dawns
Shall ye be whole. Behold me, I am strong.
And when the satrap healed has gone away
Another morrow comes, and one again.
And on these mornings will I bear ye in
Ere yet the crowd can pass. For now mine arms
Can smite the rabble back, and ye shall live
In healthful strength, lo, yet these many years.
Into the sunlight passed he.

     Never yet
Had sunshine been so bright to us who stayed
Counting the hours 'till he should come again.
But nevermore his shadow on the stones
Did we behold. A Thracian troop went by,
'Twas so they told us, as he trod the street
In all his new born vigor. With the sound
Of the shrill trumpet all his heart was filled.
His eyes were dazzled with the shine of spears

And glitter of the mail. The heavy tread
In measured time allured his footsteps on:
A shrewd centurion called him, as he came
With mimic martial air, persuading him
That he should be a warrior. So, the path
That led unto the pool he knew no more.

We missed his boyish converse and were sad
That he forsook us in our dreary need;
And, lonelier still, each nearer drew to each
In sympathy of sorrow. Each with each
Had thoughts the same. 'Though we together sought
To make the burden on our hearts more light,
The years were longer and the days more dark;
We heeded not the changes of the hours.
Nor recked we of the news the gossips brought.
The alms grew scantier and the looks more cold;
Full fourscore years the widow now had known,
And I was old with weariness of time.

She spake not of to-day or yesterday,
But oft repeated she the stories o'er
Of her own youth and childhood. How she wrought,
In patient trustfulness, of garlands fair
That fell in fragments when unto her brow
She fain would lift them: and how oftentimes
They likened her to the gazelle that springs
On Sinai's desert borders. How she saw,
One drowsy eve, the camels winding come
To where the fountain flowed; and how she met
The camel driver there as once, she said,
Beside the well Rebecca found her lord.
And how she wedded. How, along the path
That led unto her dwelling, citrons trailed
Their golden fruit wherewith the children played.
How, suddenly, there came the deadly plague
And smote them all, save her. How, desolate,
With her own hands she digged the graves, and laid
The sun-parched turf upon their quiet breasts.
Then would she sit and rock her to and fro,

With low, soft moanings, and with crooning words,
And hands upon her knees and arms half bent
As if the dead they cradled in their fold.
Sometimes in dazed imaginings she said
Her children waited for her in the vale
Beyond the mountains: that their voices cried
Upon the slow winds, asking she should come.

The months grew longer than the years had been,
And fair sweet days of evanescent spring
More dull than first had seemed the latter rain,
When gloomy vapors filled the narrow street.
Our home had grown the arches, and the dark
And starlight of the night beheld us there.
The widow, on a mat of woven reeds
Grown on Abana's edges, hid herself
Behind the pillars for her restless sleep.
I, in the outer porch on sackcloth couch
A water bearer gave me when the pool
The bruises of a fray had healed for him.

And oftentimes the nights were cold and we
Cared not to see to-morrow. Oftentimes
The dogs from out the city lanes stole near,
And with damp nostrils touched our sleeping eyes,
Then finding us alive gave yell and shrank
With crouching haunches into dark again.

At last a morning came, and I, alone,
Gazed on the shimmering water in the ray
Of the last starlight.

    For when midnight came
I heard a low voice call me and I woke.
She knelt beside me and within her eyes
A glad light shone. Her aged face was fair
With smiling calm and peace ineffable.

Behold! she said, an Angel I have seen.
Yea, He who stirs the pool. I waking lay
Watching the thin clouds drift across the sky

To hide the stars and send them forth again;
When suddenly a Presence near me stood,
Clad in white raiment and with folded hands,
And sandals flecked with grains of desert dust.
Around his head a halo of soft light,
Yet not of sun or star, but like the glow
A distant beacon launches to the sky
From some far hillside hidden from our sight.
And there was kindness in his eyes, and strength
In all his limbs, and thought was on his brow;
And a sweet sadness played around his mouth.
In his low voice was all the melody
Of holy chanting heard from aisles afar;
Yet breathing simple words. What wouldst thou have?
He asked of me; and pleading I replied:

Oh! Gentle Master, I would have the days
Of peaceful rest that knew me long ago,
When I a child beside the fountain played
And wove me garlands of the early flowers.

Aye, kind, good Master, I would know again
The joy that in the twilight came to me
To watch the camels coming one by one
Along the winding road, the peace I knew
When I in ashes baked the millet bread
For him who ruled our home. Yea, give to me
Oh, Blessed Lord, the voices that I heard
My little children speak so long ago.
Yea, Master, if I go beyond the hills
There shall I find them. I am weak and old
But if the pool but heal me I shall go.
I left them there and they are waiting me
And wondering why I come not unto them.
But I am broken now and all my frame
Is weariness and woe. When comes the dawn,
Into the pool, oh, Master, bear me in
That I, made strong, may yet return to them.

The while I prayed the halo round His head
With deeper luster shone. In lordlier guise

His snowy raiment flowed. His gaze more deep
Sank searching into mine—until, afeard,
I dropt mine eyes and listened. Yea, I heard.
So shall it be, He said, and when the dawn
Shall shine upon the ripples thou shalt know
All this thou askest. Then a little while
I waited in the silence. When I looked,
Lo, He was gone.

     Then, thinking she had dreamed,
But seeking still to comfort her, I said
Yea, sister, it is well, rejoice and hope,
And rest until the morning. We shall see—
But ere my words were ended, slow her eyes
Closed in a peaceful sleep. Upon her lips
A sweet smile played as if a pleasant thought
Too tired for utterance had lingered there.
And as a child will lay its drowsy head
Upon a grassy bank or sloping knoll,
So laid she down her forehead on my breast

And answered not my words. Nor evermore
Knew she of earth the weariness and woe.

He is alone who hath no friend anear
Although earth's hosts were marshalled at his side.
And I, alone, while other years went by
Recked not their course, or heeded what they brought
Of shine or shadow to the outer world.
And so it happed one morn I brooding lay:
Whereon One spake, in snowy raiment clad,
How long, oh, man, art thou abiding here
And wherefore seek'st thou not the troubled wave
Thence passing forth rejoicing. Lo, I cried
In bitterness of heart, can these weak limbs
Wrestle with all the crowd? How, poor and old,
Shall I find bearers when the waters rise?
My trembling limbs are bruiséd by the stress
Of many jostling feet. Here, thirty years
And eight have laid their lash upon my brow
In groove and wrinkle, and abiding snow

Is on my beard. The mockers mock at me
With spurning thrust and rudely uttered jest,
And bid me seek for healing in the pool.

And as I, angered, answered, from His eyes
A soft clear light outshone. Around His head
The morning rays seemed bended to a crown.
In majesty He stood. His vesture white
With graceful folds descended to His feet
Whereon were sandals reddened by the touch
Of the dun desert pathways; and His hands
As dove's wings waver low above the cote
Waver'd above my head as if to bless.
The while He spake in accents vibrant, clear,
Commanding as the brazen trumpet's blast,
Yet kindly as the viols dulcet sound:
Arise and take thy bed and hence depart
Thy heavy penance done; thy sin atoned:
And breathe again the glory of the air
That sweeps among the hills, and in the vales

Sleeps stilly in the sun.   Then He was gone
Ere yet the import of His words I knew.

Through all my veins there came a glow of strength,
And my dim eyesight cleared, so I could see
Of distant birds the flight, and at my feet
The little red ants crawling in the dust.
And then, as I was bidden, forth I went
Into the outer day.   The narrow street
To me was golden in the mellow morn,
And all things fair and sweet and full of peace.

Above the wall the myrtle's starry blooms,
And dark leaves tremulous on slender sprays,
Recalled the path to Hebron, and I passed
Out through the gate and southward went my way
With sturdy steps and firm, with nostrils wide
Inhaling with deep breath the cheery air.
And when the noon drew nearer and the heat
Brought languor to my feet, I loitered slow
And sought amid the herbage that I trod

For herbs to please my senses. There I found
Rare mandrakes that, divided, semblance gave
Of bearded faces in their cloven walls:
That cried as from the earth I drew them forth,
So I might eat them with a cloying tongue.
I from the mallow gathered musky seeds
Rejoicing in their odor.

                Then mine eyes
Recalled once more the beauty of the flowers,
Of lilies, and of Sharon's daffodils,
And roses of Damascus purple strown.
The storax branches bearing blooms of snow
Out-thrown from leaves, that swaying in the wind,
Showed white and green alternate. And mine ear,
Having its share of all the joyous toil
Of knowing earth again, took heed and heard
The warble of the song thrush and the lark;
And from the olive groves the bulbul's note
In full-toned melody.

            But taking heed
That fast the hours were wasting, on I trod
With measured step and steady. Soon I saw
The sparrows sit alone upon the rocks,
And solitary storks on loftiest trees
By low, rude dwellings, at whose open doors
The women sat and sang, beside the mills
Slow turned to grind the corn, although the sun
Was speeding to the west. From this I knew
That Hebron lay a little way before;
Fair Hebron, with her vineyards and her palms!
But, wearied with my journey, loitering,
I sought for fallen dates; and 'neath an oak
Lay down and slept, and when I startled woke
The stars had risen, and the early night
Was calm and clear.

                        Across the silent air
A shawm's loud blast rose strident and anear;
In lower tones came tinkling of a harp.

So, from this token, by the well, I knew
The dancers made them merry in the eve.

Then I forgot the eight and thirty years
Since I the wine-gourd drained beside the spring,
And all my outworn raiment, and my beard
Grown white as citron blossoms in the spring.
And when I, joyous, joined it, all the crowd
Had gibe, and laugh, and little wanton jest
Wherewith to vex me: Will the old man dance?
Cried one, her hair unsnooded, and her arms,
Each gentle curve displaying, on my neck.
Whereat they shouted lustily and sang
Rude songs to further laughter, till awaked
To all the change in me, I felt mine eyes
The unresisted tears drop slowly down,
So that they ceased, abashed. Oh, youths! I said,
And joyous maidens! Life and love are sweet
As sounds of music in the silent night.
But night and music vanish, and the joy

Is ended in its time. An hour to dance,
And yet an hour to sing, was said of old
When wise men taught our fathers. Let the song
And cadence of the viol charm the night
Ere yet the days of evil come, when ye
May find no pleasure in them! On each head
The old man leaves his blessing and departs.

But lonelier than of old, when I beheld
The idle leaves adrift upon the pool,
I went my way into the outer fields,
Nor cared to seek the town. Where melons grew
I found a hut on sturdy stakes upraised
Above the vapors of the teeming earth;
Its ragged thatch gave shelter till the morn.
And now, I said, Engedi's fount is far,
But it shall I behold ere sunset falls.

Then with free feet I trod the winding path
In cool of morning, and in noontide glow.

I gathered herbs that in the meadows grew.
And fruits from branches shaken by the breeze.
By wayside springs I knelt for pleasant draughts,
And peace was in my heart, such peace as knows
The bird free flown in air, or lizard lain
In safe luxuriance in the sultry sun.
Yea, more than this, before me on my way
A scorpion lay unfolded, yet the staff
Within my hand forebore to injure him,
And stepping quick aside I left him there;
Rejoicing that with me he knew the warmth
And shared with me the glory of the day.
At last I saw a shadow trailing far
Where a fair palm rose stalwart 'gainst the sky,
Grown crimson in the west; I sought the well
But was a stranger as I leaned and gazed
Into its limpid depths. The clouds, the same
As in the olden time, inverted there
Swam gently on in silence, and the moss,
As long ago, grew on the inner wall.

But rank weeds were on all the earth around,
The curb was broken and the hyssop gone.

Then on my heart came weariness, and fain
I was to weep. For all were gone away
That once I knew nor could I follow them.
Nor was there any one to seek for me.
A drowsy bee droned past me and I said
He seeks the crevice of the aged tree,
Where mid the mould and odors of decay
He findeth his own home and knoweth it.
So let me see the porches once again,
And old familiar sights, and hear the sounds
Of all the turmoil of the city streets.
So while the stars were shining, steadily
I trod the way toward Jerusalem,
And reached it at the dawn; but in an hour
I tired me of the pool. The temple wall
Was close beside and in the neighb'ring street,
I sought its shadow in the sultry noon.

Beside the southern wall there graceful leaned
A woman, one of Cyprus, with her hair
In jetty curls on ivory shoulders thrown;
With laughing eyes and with her rounded breasts
Half shown by drooping of the careless robe,
And with crushed camphire sweet and redolent,
Beside her feet a wine jar: in her hand
A taper cup of beryl.   And she sang,
Low voiced and clear, a soft alluring song.

Oh.   Drink the wine and it will banish care,
And he that is alone shall need no friend;
He that is old shall have his youth again.
To him that drinks the wine new love shall come,
And he whose heart is cold shall fervent find
The red blood running warm within his veins.
For him the curtains wove of orient weft,
Their broidered folds shall sway in gentle airs.
For him the henna's snowy cups of bloom
Shall give their odor forth.   Oh. Drink the wine,

And discontent shall vanish as the dew
On Hermon fades before the breath of morn.

From loneliness to mirth were precious change.
With eager hand I reached to grasp the cup,
The gay song answering with gayer jest,
And ardent gaze on all the loveliness
Her loosened robe disclosed. When suddenly,
Beware, I heard in accents deep and strong
As bid an arm upraised for evil deed,
At once be stayed. Then knelt I at the feet
Of Him who broke my bonds beside the pool,
And cried, Oh, Abba, pardon, and the hem
Of his white garment lifted to my lips,
Fearing to raise mine eyes or see His face,
Or hearken to his words of righteous wrath.
Beware, He said. Have I not borne thy woe,
And all thy sin from which thy woe outsprang:
Sending thee forth rejoicing as of old
When earth was fair to thee and youth was thine.

Then carefully take heed lest thou return
Into thine old abasement and no help
Unto thy misery come evermore—
For mark thee, as the olive when its stem
Is worn and old and bears but withered leaves,
And falls beneath the burden of the wind,
Is grown again from never dying root;
So in the far hereafter shalt thou rise
From thine old self of good or evil done.
And verily I tell thee: They who mourn
Shall comfort find, and all the humble share
Jehovah's kingdom: and the merciful
Have mercy for themselves. The earth shall yield
Its blessings to the debonnair, and they
Who bear pure hearts with their own eyes behold
The ever living God.

Then He was gone.
The traffickers passed by me, each intent
On his own errand. Low the Cypriote sang

Her song persuasive in alluring tones
To one from Lebanon, a mountaineer,
Nor on me glanced again. Amid the throng
I found no comforting or thought of calm.

The burning sun shone on the narrow streets,
And drowsiness was brooding in the air;
While sullen sultriness within my veins
Crept slow and venomed; and my brain was dulled,
And my faint heart was weary. Dreamily
I communed with myself: Lo! I was made
By Him who made the world. He made me thus,
And wherefore on me lies the heavy load
Of stern denial to the thoughts He gave,
And all resistance to temptations sent
In pleasant guise to make my days more fair,
And make more sweet the life He gave to me;
Yea, this, my life, whose wasting autumn comes
With something of the summer in its fold?

While pondering thus I lingered where were sold
The spices of the East, and strange perfumes
Won from the herbs of many distant lands;
And while I loitered, timid drew anear,
From out the alien crowd, a form I knew;
For sure none other had so graceful mien,
Or bore such wealth of beauty in her hair —
Sable as are the wings of birds that slay
The swarming locusts on far Shinar's plains—
Massive upon her shoulders, and, adown,
Its fringes clinging to the flexile knee.
Aye! She it was, and yet I scarcely kenned
That it could be, so strangely was she changed;
For high unto her throat there clung her robe,
Wrapped careful on the rounded breast, and all
Its loveliness concealed. Her step no more
Was careless in its grace; the longing eyes
Were mild as with the fire the starlight gives
To the calm skies of harvest, and her mouth
Was innocent as lips of childhood are,

That know nor scorn, nor anger or of guile,
Or any thought of wrong; and sweeter, far,
Than when she sang of roses was her voice,
Low-toned and tremulous, the while she asked:
Hast thou rich spikenard—that which traders bring
From the far plains beyond the purple sea,
Sealed in the lucent kists of shining stone?
And here is gold to pay its price withal.

At this the merchant laughed: Who hast thou snared,
That he should scatter gold as leaves are blown,
Or olives shaken from the autumn branch?
And so from out thy curtains must the breath
Of costliest perfumes waver on the night;
Thy couch more odorous than all the fields
On Sharon's slopes, where amorous roses grow!
I would, he said, that I were but a girl,
And not a trader in these costly wares,
So I might gather gold with luring looks
And dulcet singing of soft songs to men.

Then over the broad forehead and the cheek
And on the gentle neck, like flush of dawn
That deepens into scarlet, came a glow.
And then, like snow upon a crimson bloom,
Came deathly pallor, and from tremulous lips
Half failing into sobbing came reply:
Thy jest is evil and thy words are naught.
These coins I earned by toiling in the fields
Where crisping wheat and sturdy barley drew
Their rasping beards across these tender hands.
The sickle wielded and the gavels bound
From early morn when on my arms there rained
From the tall grain the cold night gathered dews.
When the sun smote me until faintness came
As from a burden heavy to be borne.
Through the hot noontides when the wheat was dry
And scattered kernels at each careless touch.
Into the twilight when, new born, the dew
Lay on the stubble; and the twisted straw
Was pliant knotted on the yielding sheaf.

Yet every day was sweet with solace wrought
In this, that all unblemished came the dole
That guerdoned my long toil. For I had will'd
To make a stainless offering to one
Unstained by earthly guile. This gold is clean
As holy is its purpose, void of wrong,
Like to the sacrifice on altars laid
By pure hands for pure hearts in olden time.
As if her tears were dropping with her words
Her low voice seemed, the while the precious kist
She laid within the raiment on her breast.
Then went upon her way with steadfast step
And calm, untroubled eyes, and cheek that paled
To dusky softness in the ardent day.

Then, curious to know, I followed her
And said, Oh, daughter, dost of roses sing
As in old days, or art thou silent now
With silence born of sorrow, for no joy
Is on thy lip, though loving peace hath laid

Her touch upon thy forehead.   Wherefore this?
I seek for rest and no rest comes to me.

There is no rest, she answered, patience comes
And is to rest as is the Rabbi's prayer
After the chanting of the rhythmic psalm:
As cool of twilight after quiet noons,
Or stillness of fair waters when their flow
Has ceased in limpid lakes.

                        Aye, Aye, Quoth I,
But wherefore patience when our wasted years
Haunt us like shadows stalking by our side,
And, mocking, point us to the void beyond.

Not so, she said.   The Nazarine doth say,
And him we trust in humbleness and faith,
That a sin offering for us shall be,
And all atonement made for evil done,
For those who in His name do ask for it.

And we, relieved from soilure of our days,
Shall purity of childhood know again:
So when the change that we call death hath come,
We pass into a realm where peace doth reign,
Whose gates are barred to sorrow, and where fear
Is ever alien, and where innocence
Disports itself in gladness in the light
That like unchanging sunrise, gilds the throne
Of God, our Father. So in faith we wait
In penitence and patience for our rest.

The while she spake a sudden uproar grew
As of a crowd pursuing, and she fled
Ere it should come to us. And as she ran
I saw her little feet like swallows skim
The stony way; her graceful limbs that swayed
Within her loosened raiment as the branch
Of some fair vine swings pendant with its leaves
Outblown by passing breezes, and her arm
Like tawny ivory bended to her breast

To hold the casket mid a gathered fold
Of drooping raven hair.

                Now all my thoughts
Were grown confused and dim. As in a dream
I saw my mother's face and heard her say
That we should rest when all of life was done,
As she had spoken ere the harvest moon
On her closed eyelids shone. Anon, I thought
Of the high mountain whence the trav'ler saw
The crimson sun at midnight rise again
To a new day withouten dark between.
And then it seemed, from patience into rest,
Was whispered in mine ear. Then rude the tale
Of the wild robber chief returned to me,
And how his woe endureth evermore;
How all of evil, more than sevenfold
After its kind doth bear of bitter fruit.
I thought of guilt and the enduring scourge
Of memory when all the joy is gone

That made its apples sweet. The Prophet's words
Came hollow sounding back; so, on and on,
Till time shall end, our deeds shall follow us,
Yet there is One who cometh. To and fro,
Like the swift shuttle in a weaver's hands,
The riddle sounded in my weary brain
Of whom it was so promised! Then to me
Came recollection of the legend old
The youth had told concerning Solomon
In his last day, when all of vanity
Was the wide past to him: when high were drawn
The curtains from the ages yet to be.
Where he beheld afar a Stronger rise,
Yea, One more wise and purer, from whose hands
Upon the poor should benediction come.

Dazed and distraught I rose and ere I knew,
I was beyond the city gates, the fields
Were green beside me.

All my heart was dust
As was the ashen way beneath my feet.
Behold, I said, there is no place for me,
And all is doubt within me and without.
An hundred days will I in deserts bide
With prayer and fasting: and in solitude
Mayhap will wisdom find a voice for me
And guidance give.

I sought the wilderness
And ate of bitter herbs; from brackish springs
I slaked my thirst, and many vigils kept.
Yet all was vain, though visions came to me,
Bloodless and cold in watches of the night,
And fiends tormenting in my loneliness.
Until the hundreth morn was come and gone,
Aye. All is vain I said, there is no light
Save of these senses, like a glowworm's spark,
Whose evil odor mingles with its ray
And marks it of the earth. Then through my brain

There shot the sensuous pleasure of the thought
Of the fleet feet whose graceful steps I saw
Flee from the crowd, a hundred days before,
And the round arm and buoyant, springing limbs.
Then, like rebuke, the memory of her face,
Chastened with sorrow, yet alight with trust,
Came o'er me as I walked, and all her words—
Forgotten until now—returned to me:
The Nazarine hath spoken. Who is he?
For out of Nazareth no good may come,
They said, when I was young. Now I am old,
And still they say the same.

                    In querulous thought
And motiveless, I wended t'ward the gates;
But ere I reached them came a traveler—
Cheery of face—and met me on the way.
The Nazarine? quoth I. And who is He?
And what His work, and where shall Him I find?
Ah! He is dead! he answered; and the crowd

Is laughing at the jest. Between two thieves
They slew Him on the cross! Jerusalem
No more is troubled with the Nazarine.

Then stunned as one, from out a dreamy sleep,
Wakes to the glare of noonday—Lo, I said,
This, too, is vain, and hope but mocks at me!

Sad sought I, then, the ford of Kedron, where
The road leads to the fields, and sat me down;
And from mid afternoon till sunset came
I pondered on my days:

      And one by one
Each old experience came back to me
Like pictures 'broidered on dark silken folds
Of curtains passed before me. At my side
There chirped a robin, borne on weary wing,
And with unwonted crimson on its breast.

'The Nazarine hath spoken!' seemed to me
As words far floating in a tender voice,
Remote and tremulous, from out the air.
Then from my arid eyelids sprang the tears,
And in meek tones I murmured: Father, Hear!
Though now it be the Nazarine is dead,
And Him I knew not with mine earthly sight,
As He hath done for Thy most favored ones,
So let Him do for me; and in His Name
And for His sake let light henceforth be mine
For guidance into rest!

                          The deepened shade
Crept down from Olivet. I shook the dust
From my worn sandals t'ward the city gates,
In purpose to depart, but loitered, still,
Uncertain whither should my footsteps go.
Softly I thought of Hebron's quiet graves,
Wherein, of old, the two I loved were laid,
And were they sunken so that alien feet

Athwart them trod, unknowing? Did the rose
Bloom by them as long since? And were the palms,
Sprung from the seeds of Egypt, stately there,
With growth unkenned by me?

Then thought more harsh
Of who had known me in the distant days
Would hail me now in Hebron, save with gibes;
How they whose grandsires knew me in my youth
Would mock my ragged garb. No more, I said,
Need I that pathway travel. Thence afar
To Emmaus or Gadara I will go;
There no man's memory may my name recall.

With purpose steadfast and unswerving feet
I hied me on my way. But scarce an hour
Was gone before I paused. A woman, bent
With weight of beggary and famished toil,
Stood by the wayside with extended hands.
No word she spake; but her dark eyes were dulled

As if by prayers unanswered, and her lips
Trembled as if with asking long denied;
Her snowy hair from wrinkled temples hung
To shrunken shoulders, and her fingers brown,
Were like the talons of the birds that come
In times of famine from the distant hills
To tear the scattered flocks. Unknown to me
Her face and figure; but familiar still,
As is a dream remembered in a dream,
Faint and elusive to our clearer thought;
And like a vision in a dream recalled
Rose mine own sorrow through the faded years,
When, from Engedi's vale, I sought the pool,
And then—in strange inconsequence—the mound
Whereon I planted seeds so long ago.
And then a consciousness within my brain
Seemed speaking silently, but heard withal:
Even as from the mellowed earth does rise
Bright palms from dusky seeds, so in thine heart
Should mercy rise from sorrow. So, I sought

Within my folded girdle. Thence I drew
The two Denarii that the noble gave,
And laid them in her hand.

     In quaver shrill
Quoth she: The Lord will bless thee, for thy hand
Is open to the poor and they are His.
And, Shobab, look on me, knowst not the child
That to her mother's garment clung the while
She gave thee sombre seeds of Egypt's palm;
Or yet the maiden who with timbrel's sound
Hailed thee, beside the path, the afternoon
Ye went returning from Jerusalem
Toward the ripened vineyards long ago;
Aye, in the distant years when we were young.
Now, we are old and time for rest is near.
So heed my words. For well my mother knew
The runes that lay within the hidden kist,
Beneath the throne of Solomon, the king
Of Judah and of Genii; and whom God

Gave wisdom greater than to Sons of men.
For God, our Father, speaks in many ways
And guides us with the shadow of His hand,
Which we deem darkness while it leads to light.
As in far Thebes the tufted pinnacles
Rear their green heads aloft, where holy ones
Shall come to dwell in solitude and calm,
So by fair Hebron's fountains rise the shafts
Of palms thy hands have planted, and their leaves
Sway gently o'er the graves of those ye loved.
There go and rest shall find thee, and content,
And placidness of thought, and peacefulness
Free from all turmoil of the stormy world;
Void of regret for all the years agone,
And fear of those that yet may come to thee.

Farewell, I answered, Sister, may His hand
Deal gently with thy age, and peace be thine
As thou hast willed for me. And as I spake

We turned and went upon our several way.
She speaketh truth I said.

     The haunts of men
Are nevermore for me; nor yet the fields
Where solitude is brooding and my heart
Aches in the void of silence. I recall
Where close by Hebron lies the narrow road,
The fountain yields its waters, and the dates
By winds that sweep o'er autumn threshing floors
Are scattered to the ground. There caravans
Of traders come and go. There some are ill,
With fevers of the desert; stricken some
With wounds from battles foughten in the plains
And fain would have of succor. I will go.
Beside the spring a dwelling rude will raise
And drive away the weeds with thrift of figs;
With opulence of melons and of corn.
There every morn of gentle toil shall bring
Its due allotted portion, and each eve

The promise of sweet sleep. Each noontide hour
Shall bear the benison of pleasant rest
Beneath the trees I planted long ago.
So, germinal of all fair thoughts shall life
Pass softly to its end, when I shall know
The unread mystery that lies beyond:
And from this flow'ring of my spirit here
Shall gather distant fruitage.

      Thence I came;
The Theban palms were buoyant in the breeze,
Their stems like pillars rose against the sky,
And, at their feet, the wild thorn-roses blew
As in my youth I knew them. Though the graves
Were leveled with the ground I kenned their place,
And close beside them seemed a space for me.
The twilight came, and darkness, yet I stayed
For whither elsewhere should I seek my home?

I sat beside the curb, a fallen stone
Rounded and smooth made pillow for my head

Bowed low on bended arms. My drowsy eyes
Closed wearily: no rest was in my heart.
The thin voice of the creeping wind came faint
Through the low herbs. It faded into tones,
For now I slept, of softly breathing flutes
Borne near and nearer. Then, through silver veils
That changed to gold and crimson in the sky,
Then cleft apart while azure shone beyond,
I saw the cherubim rise from the ark—
The carven ark, that 'neath the temple roof,
I saw lang syne—and from their lips there came
Joining the slender music, joyous song.

It is no dream, they sang; for God hath raised
Beyond earth's darkened realm His palaces
Wherein earth's sons and daughters strive no more
With sorrow or with wrong. There love is fond
Yet hath no passion; and there, gentleness
Hath fear of no beguiling. Innocence,
That knows no craft, is shining in each face;

And unto each his childhood comes again,
Blent with the wisdom that his pilgrimage,
Or brief or long, hath taught him.

      So they sang.
And then, as if receding, sang again.
It is no dream, they sang; it is no dream.
Then as in silence their sweet voices died
The azure cloud was lifted, and below
I saw broad gardens. Mid the leafy shade
Arose the domes of temples; and the air
Was sweet and hazy with an incense smoke
That rose unceasing to a hidden throne,
Known by its soft effulgence thrown afar
On the high skies. And in those fields beheld
A little maid adorned with daffodils
And coiling roses on her shoulders thrown.
A dark face, sable bearded, on whose brow
The helmet's mark seemed graven. More than all,
Crowned with ripe wheat that white as lilies shone,

My fair young mother, for from her was gone
All that which was of sorrow or of toil.
Yea, those I knew beside the distant pool
Were there with them, and peace was with them all.

I woke. The chill wind through the herbage crept:
Coldly the starlight shone. The branchéd palms
Threw far and clear a tracery of shade
That wavered on the ground. But, at its edge,
The sky bore silver promise of the dawn.

Where reached the shadows when the sunrise came.
I builded these stone walls beside the path,
Upon them laid this roof of verdant turf;
This garden digged where wanton weeds were grown.
With mine own feet through yonder herbage wore
The gray line of the path that meets the track
That, through the vale, the traders traverse slow.
Here have I borne the weary to my home,
And here have carried to wayfaring ones

Of cooling water and of welcome food—
Have knelt beside the dying; of the dead
The wearied eyes have closed: and they who mourned,
With words of comforting have lulled to sleep.

So, in the change of never changing days,
Long since came perfect peace.

     But yester-eve
A new-found glory kindled all my heart
With an exultant joy. A Canaanite
Asked of me shelter, and beside my hearth
Gazed keen into my face. Ah! Thou art he,
He said, who long ago beside the pool
Beneath the porches, at the Master's word
Arose and walked, and bore thy bed away,
Though not for thee the troubled waters rose.
And knowst thou not the Master? He who lay
Within the manger when the fleecy light
Made aureole on the Virgin Mother's head;

He who to Egypt fled from Herod's wrath,
And slept beneath a palm whose branch shall wave
When dawns the Last Day on the earth redeemed.
He whom they crucified on Calvary
That even I, a Gibeonite, should live
Free from the sin atoned for by His Blood.
Yea; Shiloh, prophesied from olden time,
Whose Kingdom is of Heaven, and whose sway
Is in men's hearts, and over all the earth
Shall spread in beams of holy blessedness.

Then knew I who had healed me, and I knelt
And invocation made. Oh, Father, hear:
Although like barren fig trees are my days,
As wirble of dead leaves on Autumn winds,
Or stubble shorn by fire, yet I am Thine;
My wrong atoned for and my burden cast
Through Him whose agony hath purchased peace
To all Thy children. Therefore bid me come
To mine inheritance beside Thy throne.

And if, Oh, Father, it may be Thy will,
Then grant a sign that I perchance may ken
When Thy call cometh and mine hour is near.

Then, from an ashen cloud that rode the sky,
A lambent light descended as a torch,
Inverted, flares a moment and is gone.
And by this symbol given, well I know
That ere yon sun is hidden in the west
My task is finished and my journey done.

FINIS.

www.ingramcontent.com/pod-product-compliance
Lightning Source LLC
Chambersburg PA
CBHW030346170426
43202CB00010B/1261